LIVING
FEARLESSLY

Books by Sheila Walsh

Bring Back the Joy
Gifts for Your Soul
Honestly
Living Fearlessly

Coauthor of

Boundless Love
Extravagant Grace
Outrageous Joy
OverJoyed

LIVING
FEARLESSLY

TELLING THE TRUTH

FACING YOUR FEARS

FINDING HIS PEACE

SHEILA WALSH

ZondervanPublishingHouse
Grand Rapids, Michigan

A Division of HarperCollins*Publishers*

We want to hear from you. Please send your comments about this book
to us in care of the address below. Thank you.

ZondervanPublishingHouse
Grand Rapids, Michigan 49530
http://www.zondervan.com

Living Fearlessly
Copyright © 2001 by Sheila Walsh

Requests for information should be addressed to:

ZondervanPublishingHouse

Grand Rapids, Michigan 49530

Library of Congress Cataloging-in-Publication Data
Walsh, Sheila, 1956-
    Living fearlessly: telling the truth, facing your fears, finding His peace / Sheila Walsh.
        p. cm.
    ISBN: 0-310-20976-5
    1. Fear—Religious aspects—Christianity. 2. Christian women—Religious life. I. Title.
BV4908.5 .W35 2001

248.8'43—dc21   00-047713
                                                                                 CIP

This edition is printed on acid-free paper.

Interior design by Todd Sprague

Printed in the United States of America

---

01 02 03 04 05 06 /❖ DC/ 10 9 8 7 6 5 4 3 2 1

This book is dedicated in loving memory of

William Otto Pfaehler
February 5, 1919–November 6, 2000
We miss you, Papa!

ACKNOWLEDGMENTS

Writing this book has changed my life. There are some special people I would like to thank.

Debbie Gibson. You have endured more human suffering than I can comprehend. You have endured it all with grace, humility, and kindness. I am proud to be your friend.

Brian and Debbie Schrauger. You have lived with every parent's nightmare. You have lived my fears. I have watched your struggle, and I've seen the tears and heard the laughter, and your faith has taught me more than I can put into words.

Taylor Schrauger. I look in the book of Hebrews and find you there: "The world was not worthy of them.... These were all commended for their faith, yet none of them received what had been promised. God had planned something better for us so that only together with us would they be made perfect."

To *all the women who so generously shared your stories* with me, thank you!

Thank you to *Sandy Vander Zicht* and the staff at Zondervan for giving me the freedom to address the issues I feel passionately about.

To my editor, *Traci Mullins,* I owe a world of thanks. You laughed and cried with me through this book. You are much more than an editor; you are a true friend and fellow pilgrim who is not afraid to ask the difficult questions we tend to whisper in the dark. I thank you, Traci, from the bottom of my heart.

CONTENTS

From My Heart ...

SAYING YES! TO GOD

Dare I lay my cards out on the table?

This book was a gift from God to my own soul. He saw in me a woman who was so afraid of many things and gave me the challenge of writing about fear in order to teach me how to live without fear. I was afraid to give an unconditional Yes! to God. What if he brought me to a darker night than I would be able to bear? What if my worst fears materialized? Would I lose faith in the goodness of God in the midst of that unspeakable agony?

I wanted to live free from fear's grip, but I didn't know how. I had become so accustomed to grasping control. It felt comfortable to me—safe. In John's Gospel we read that "the truth will set you free." But it also holds you accountable to live according to this freeing truth. If you lived inside your house all your life and never knew there was a world outside, that would be sad. But if, having once been outside those four walls, you stayed locked inside, that would be tragic.

I have tasted enough of truth and freedom to know that I want to live outside of my self-imposed prisons of fear. Perhaps you have too. I believe that God wants us to live a life of freedom based not on what we judge is "safe," but on the unshakable foundation of who he is.

A DIARY OF THE SOUL

—Night is drawing nigh—
For all that has been—Thanks!
For all that shall be—Yes!

These challenging words were found in a manuscript in the home of Dag Hammarskjöld after he died. He was Secretary-General of the United Nations from 1953 until his untimely death in an airplane crash in 1961. Ironically, he was flying to Rhodesia to negotiate a peace settlement between the United Nations and the Katanga forces when he died.

With his last manuscript, which came to be titled *Markings*, he left a cover letter addressed to his friend, Leif Belfrage. Hammarskjöld described the contents of this book as "a sort of white book concerning my negotiations with myself—and with God." He asked his friend to determine if there was anything of value, and, if so, to have it published.

The manuscript reads like a diary of the soul, with entries dating from 1925 to a final poem Hammarskjöld wrote in 1961—just weeks before his death. He was twenty years old when he began to record his thoughts. It's exciting to follow the spiritual journey that seemed to intensify for him in the 1940s and '50s. In 1953 he wrote the words that made me want to live differently:

For all that has been—Thanks!
For all that shall be—Yes!

I read this quote in *Christianity Today* in 1998, and I couldn't get it out of my mind. Initially I wrote it down in my diary in the first blush of something that sounded "holy" and "good" and "right." But the more I came back to it, the less appealing it was. "Thanks!" for *everything?* "Yes!" to *everything?*

I needed to know more about this man and his journey, so I bought my own copy of *Markings*. As I traced Hammarskjöld's path, I found that he left some clear markers for me to follow:

> Hallowed be thy name,
>> not mine.
> Thy kingdom come,
>> not mine.
> Thy will be done,
>> not mine.

Scottish preacher William Barclay writes that Jesus is the yes to every promise of God. I hear this as the ultimate surrender of control to a loving and trustworthy Father. Perhaps that's the turning point: finding out who it is we are saying yes to. Surely it would revolutionize everything if we grasped the One we are being asked to say yes to and the liberty that comes from finally unclenching our fist and putting our hand into God's hand.

In the journey through the valley of my own fears, God has brought some wonderful people into my life. They have lived my greatest nightmares and yet have been soaked to the soul in the grace of God in ways that make no sense apart from him. Those who have had their hearts broken and soothed by God can give to others a compassion and a wisdom that defies human understanding.

David the psalmist is such a person. In Psalm 102:4–7 we find these haunting words:

> My heart is blighted and withered like grass;
>> I forget to eat my food.
> Because of my loud groaning
>> I am reduced to skin and bones.
> I am like a desert owl,
>> like an owl among the ruins.
> I lie awake; I have become
>> like a bird alone on a roof.

Yet just a few verses later (verses 18–20) he writes:

Let this be written for a future generation,
    that a people not yet created may praise the LORD:
"The LORD looked down from his sanctuary on high,
    from heaven he viewed the earth,
to hear the groans of the prisoners
    and release those condemned to death."

David spoke the truth to God. He poured out his pain and his questions. He agonized over the sin that cast a dark cloud over his soul. Yet, in the midst of his darkest moments, there are gifts of grace. Pearls of peace. The unmistakable melody of utter confidence in the love and mercy of God. A song of faith, calling us to trust God in the darkness, "that a people not yet created may praise the LORD." *A people not yet created.* That's you and me—those who trace our heritage of faith back to this distant brother.

Facing our deepest fears means making peace with our seen self and with our unseen self.

David spoke the truth. He faced his fears head-on, and following that authentic path led him to receive the gift of peace. I believe that deep, abiding peace is possible only when all our cards are on the table before the Lord. I'm convinced that we can't be at peace if we are attempting to hide our true selves from God. Facing our deepest fears means making peace with our *seen self* and with our *unseen self.* We all have both.

For me, there is the Sheila Walsh my friends and family know well. There is the Sheila Walsh the public knows pretty well too. And then there is another me. She is made up of all my unspoken thoughts, terrors, temptations, and private rebellions. I am learning to bring *all* the parts of me into God's presence, into the circle of his embrace, because I have become convinced that this is the only path to peace.

This journey has changed my life. I finished this book a different woman than the one who began it. Only God could have worked such a transformation. He can do the same in you if you are willing to tell him the truth—the whole truth about you, which he knows already. Because his mercies are new *every* morning, you can find the courage to bring all of who you are to all of who he is. You can face your fears head-on. You can find the peace that transcends all understanding.

"There is no fear in love. But perfect love drives out fear" (1 John 4:18). Will you come along with me on the journey toward living fearlessly?

Part 1

TELLING THE TRUTH

A Fearful Prayer

Dear God,

I want to love you with my whole heart. I want to trust you, but I'm afraid. I'm afraid I'll lose control—and then anything could happen. I wonder what you'll ask me to do to prove that I love you or what you might take away from me and how painful will it be. I want to change, but I don't know how. I know you know that. Please help me. Please do it gently.

Your daughter,
Sheila

1

CONFESSIONS OF A
CONTROL FREAK

Men who fear God face life fearlessly. Men who do not fear God end up fearing everything.

Richard Halverson

The LORD is my light and my salvation—
whom shall I fear?
The LORD is the stronghold of my life—
of whom shall I be afraid?

Psalm 27:1

Forgive us our lack of faith, lest ulcers become our badge of disbelief.
Peter Marshall

I'm afraid of losing control

It was supposed to be a perfect day! I had been looking forward to it for a whole week. My husband, Barry, and I had been married on December 3, and now we were going to buy our first Christmas tree together.

I don't tend to think of myself as an off-the-chart romantic. I don't read romance novels. I'd rather see a suspenseful drama than a romantic movie any day of the week. But when the Christmas season rolls around I turn to mush. My husband had no idea what he was signing up for.

The day after Thanksgiving I dig out my favorite Christmas CD collection. The sounds of Andy Williams, Bing Crosby, Nat King Cole, The King's College Choir, The

Carpenters, and those wonderful Irish boys, The Chieftains, fill my home and my car until every last ho! ho! ho! is silenced for another year. I lovingly place my stack of Christmas videos next to the VCR, like a gift at the manger. I watch each one at least once. I start with *Miracle on 34th Street*—the original, then the remake. I move to *A Christmas Story* with the Red Ryder BB gun, and follow up with *Prancer* and *A Charlie Brown Christmas*. Then comes the "hug-your-family movie," *It's a Wonderful Life*. I make a fresh commitment to live my life to the fullest and never be mean to my husband again. (I also make a mental note to never give the bank deposit to my uncle on Christmas Eve.)

I save the best for last. I wait for a snowy day, which when I lived in California was a frustrating and fruitless wait. Now, however, Nashville will often come through for me. I gather the family. I make hot apple cider with cinnamon sticks and cloves and then light enough candles to land a small plane by. We have a moment of silence to prepare ourselves to receive. I push PLAY. There it is: *Frosty the Snowman*. I usually watch *Frosty* at least twice and am suitably devastated each time he melts.

For our first Christmas as husband and wife, I was determined that Barry and I would have an extra-special holiday season. Ho, ho, ho! I had love and Christmas tied up with a red velvet bow. Joy to the world! Barry and I drove to the tree lot at the local Presbyterian church. They were selling trees to raise funds for their youth programs, which made it almost like tithing.

"Let's get a really big one," I said as we got out of the car.

"Sure, Babe," Barry said.

We wandered up and down aisles of trees of every shape and size. "Look at this one!" I cried. "It's perfect."

"Honey, it's four feet taller than our ceiling," Barry lovingly pointed out.

"Oh. . . . What about this one?" I asked hopefully.

"It's great," he answered, "as long as you're willing to move most of our furniture into the garage until the tree dies."

I looked at the tree and had to admit that it had the circumference of a small building.

Finally we found *the* tree. We put it in the trunk of our car, tied it down, and headed home. In my mind I knew how it was going to look. I knew where every ornament was going to go. I forgot that Barry loved Christmas, too, and had brought his own fancy-shmancy decorations into my perfect Christmas. Things went downhill fast.

"That's the wrong angel!" I said, as Barry put *his* angel on the top of the tree.

"That's where I've always put it," he replied.

"But that was before we had *my* perfect angel," I pointed out.

It got a lot worse. Barry is a perfectionist. He got out the measuring tape to make sure the ornaments were hanging equidistantly from each other.

"You are a total loony!" I said. "No one measures the distance between ornaments. I'm going to tell your mom!"

It was Showdown at High Noon. On one side of the tree, a controlling Christmas romantic and, on the other, an anal perfectionist.

"This is all wrong!" I yelled, in keeping with the spirit of Christmas, tears pouring down my cheeks.

"This is the way it has to be," he said.

"This is supposed to be about joy to the world and peace on earth and goodwill to your wife," I wailed. "You've ruined Christmas! You can take your perfect tree and shove it up your perfect sweater!" I cried before running into the bathroom and slamming the door.

I sat on the toilet for a while, thinking that I'd married the wrong man and that I'd never buy another tree. From now on I'd just help the homeless and give them my entire CD and video collection. I'd hold on to *Frosty*, though. The story would just upset the homeless.

Then it hit me like a four-year-old fruitcake. I would never have believed it from anyone else. But it was Sheila Walsh talking to Sheila Walsh, and I am learning to be very honest with myself, so I paid attention. It was one of those moments—a sort of "Eureka!"

"I am a control freak."

There. I said it!

I can hardly type it now, five years later. I fumble over the spelling. I ask myself if I'm getting enough sleep. After all, I'm forty-three years old with a two-and-a-half-year-old son, so my brain cells are not all accounted for. I sing all five verses of *Amazing Grace*. But before the echoes subside, it's there again, and I know it's true: "I am a control freak."

> *"I am a control freak." There. I said it!*

Surely not! I am a darling Christian woman! I love others. I love God. I am a gentle servant of Christ, an earthen vessel, a veritable conduit of the love of God. But this had such an authentic ring to it. It had the melody, the winsomeness of truth.

I recall other moments. The times I've gone to the movies with friends and we've stood outside debating what to see. No one can make up his or her mind, so I always jump in and decide for everyone. I try to justify it in my own mind: "Some people just can't make a decision. They need people like me!" I've never put this conclusion to a vote, however.

Okay, another confession: I'm also a backseat driver. "You're too close to the car in front! You're going too fast. You didn't look before you pulled out into that lane."

It's not just me. I see it in Barry too.

"Why don't you wear that dress tonight?" he says.

"I'd rather wear a pantsuit," I answer, not admitting I feel fat in that dress or I forgot to shave my legs or I've got fifteen bruises from playing soccer in the yard with our son and unless I wear orthopedic hose, they'll show. But Barry is mad all evening because I didn't do it his way.

I've seen it in our son, Christian.

"I want to paint now, Mommy."

"We'll paint later, darling," I reply. "Right now it's time for your nap."

He throws his paintbrush across the kitchen, lies down on the floor, and screams the primal scream of every two-year-old who can't have things his way.

As human beings we control in so many ways. We try to control our spouses, our children, our friends, the way things are run at church or at the office. We love to have things our way. But it's more than that, isn't it? We feel we *need* to have things our way. Being in control makes us feel safe. Or at least it gives us the illusion of safety.

I have spent most of my life grabbing control of every situation I could in a feeble and futile attempt to shore up the rocky foundation of my life. It has never worked. It has never made me happy. It has never brought true peace. But like a moth drawn to the flame of its own destruction, I have kept flying back. I see a picture of *myself* when my son and I watch Disney's *A Bug's Life* for the five-hundredth time. One moth is talking to another. "Stay away from the light!" he cries. "But it's so beautiful!" the kamikaze moth replies just before he's zapped.

WHISPERS IN GOD'S EAR

If you had asked me, when I was the cohost of *The 700 Club*, "Sheila, do you trust God?" I would have said, "Yes. Of course I do." Wasn't that in the contract? I'm on Christian television; I must trust God. But I didn't. I wanted to. I desperately wanted to. But I was too afraid.

I didn't know that then. I had no idea how many of my decisions and actions sprang up out of fear. My behavior was so instinctual, it seemed right. I saw others around me as controlling, but I never saw it in myself.

But God is good. He took one of my greatest fears and turned it into the greatest opportunity for positive change. When I crash-landed in a psychiatric hospital, diagnosed with clinical depression, I woke up to the truth about my life. In the weeks leading up to that awful day in October of 1992 when I checked myself into the Northern Virginia Doctor's Hospital, I felt as though the walls were closing in on me. I was literally sick with anxiety, but I didn't know why. It felt more suffocating than fear. It was dread. Yet it seemed ridiculous to me. It felt as though I had some horrific skeleton in my closet and I was just waiting for the *National Enquirer* to "out" me. But my closet was fairly empty, so why this sick-to-the-pit-of-my-stomach fright? No answers.

Then one day my psychiatrist, Dr. Walter Byrd, asked me, "What are you so afraid of, Sheila?"

"I have no idea," I replied. And that was true.

"What's the worst thing that could happen to you?"

I started to say the first thing that came to my mind—"I'll lose my ministry if people know I've been a patient here." But I knew this was not the real answer. I could live with that. I just didn't know what the real answer was.

Eventually I discovered that my greatest fear was losing the control I perceived I had over my life. As God stripped away all my protective layers I found underneath it all a scared little girl who wasn't sure she could trust anyone. Growing up without a dad from the age of four onward left me feeling vulnerable, as though there were no "big person" to stick up for me. To a child death is a hole—a bottomless pit into which anyone could fall at any minute. Every room of the house echoes with unvoiced questions: *Was this my fault? If I'd remembered to tidy my room last night, would this still have happened? Mommy, are you next?*

At age thirty-five, all my greatest fears burst the walls of my "safe" little life all at one time. I couldn't imagine anything worse than being in a psychiatric ward. That's where my daddy died. Now it was my turn. My fears checked in along with me, slithering under the door:

- I was in a locked ward, with no control over anything.
- As far as I could tell, my ministry, which was my identity, was gone.
- My years of hiding behind the "perfect Christian woman" image were over.
- My desperate need to be approved of by others in order to feel good about myself lay bleeding on the floor.

It was the end. I saw that clearly. What I missed at first was that it was also the beginning. It was the beginning of the life that I had longed to live—free of paralyzing fear, not afraid to return God's smile lest he take it as a yes to serving as Mother Sheila in India.

I see this kind of freedom in my son. I learn so much from this darling lamb who, now that he is a toddler, is ninety percent angel, ten percent demon-possessed. I watch him leap off the sofa just *knowing* I'll catch him, even when my arms are full of laundry. He has absolute confidence in my trustworthiness. Absolute freedom from fear.

That's where I want to be with God. I want my life to be a faith-filled leap into his arms, knowing he will be there—not that everything will go as I want, but that *he will be there* and that this will be enough.

I don't say this lightly. I'm not that brave yet. But this is where I start. I start with my fear. I start with the fact that at times my fears are so great I can't even speak them aloud. It feels as if to do so would make them more real. If I'm really honest about what frightens me, will I be consumed by anxiety? Perhaps you understand what I'm talking about. Perhaps the very thought of being honest about your fears is terrifying.

When Christian is afraid, I notice that he whispers. If he has something to tell me that he perceives is "bad," he whispers it in my ear. To him it seems less scary if it's quiet.

- Is there a beast under my bed?
- Did I do a bad thing, Mommy?
- Did Nana die?
- Will you leave too?

It seems like a good place to start. When we cannot speak our fears out loud, perhaps we could whisper them to God. While I want to live as someone who can shout a resounding Yes! to everything God allows to come my way, I'm not there yet.

Fear is a strange wind. It is not a wind that propels us forward, but a wild paralyzing one that puts us in a holding pattern. We can't move. We can't fly backward or forward. We are stuck, held fast. I want to be free to be the whole woman God has created me to be, but I can't begin this journey until I can acknowledge my fears, until I can face what is actually true rather than what I *wish* were true about me.

As I look at my life and my years of trying to control everything around me, I know now that underneath this loud voice of control is the silent scream of fear. Take my backseat driving, for example. On the surface it looks like a nagging wife trying to tell her husband how to drive. But it's more than that. What I feel during these moments of outwardly controlling behavior is fear. I'm afraid we'll crash. I'm afraid that Barry isn't concentrating on what he's doing, so my fear makes me want to grab the wheel.

Fear is one of the most primal human emotions. I don't know if it comes with the package of our humanity or if we learn it from bad experiences in our childhood. But it's the worst backseat driver of all because it's

> *Fear is a strange wind. It is not a wind that propels us forward, but a wild paralyzing one that puts us in a holding pattern.*

never quiet; it's never just looking out the window, silently admiring the view.

Think back to your school days. I don't know about you, but I hated being a teenager. I had greasy hair and huge zits, and I was chunky. I was so chunky you could have shown *Ben Hur* on my rear end—and that's one long movie! I didn't fit in. I was the one at parties who changed the records (yes, it was records back then!). My mom made me wear "sensible" (otherwise known as big and ugly) shoes. She said I'd thank her when I grew up. I think that's why, if you looked in my closet now, you'd see that almost all of my shoes have four-inch heels. I buy the shoes about which even the salesgirl ringing up my purchase is thinking, *Man, I never thought we'd sell these ridiculous things.* If she excuses herself to go into the back room for a moment, I just know she's calling my mother!

We all wanted to be part of the "in crowd" as children, but maybe we weren't hip enough or we didn't dress the right way or we were too fat, too tall, too skinny. So we built walls around our hearts to protect us from the pain of life. We found little areas of life we could control, and we hung on to them for dear life. We ate too much or wouldn't eat at all. We talked too much or refused to join in.

But then we discovered that these walls and private rooms that became home for us also stand between us and God. We've pasted on to God our human experiences, and that's why we're so afraid of saying yes to him. He might make us do something we don't want to do or something we're afraid of. He might make us wear sensible shoes for the rest of our lives.

All through my teenage years and into my early twenties, I was sure God wanted me to be a missionary to India. It's not that I heard a specific call; I just couldn't think of anything I'd hate more. I saw myself clearly: I was standing outside a run-down shack, which was my house. My hair was a mess because there was nowhere to plug in my hair dryer. A man-eating snake was about to attack me. But that wasn't the worst of it. I had on sensible shoes. The brown lace-up kind.

I've come a long way in discovering the true heart and character of God. Now I know he's not out to ruin my life, so I'm relaxing the hold I have on many things. But I still have people and circumstances I try to control for dear life. My son is the most deeply felt one. I know I don't own my child. I know that ultimately his life is in God's hands. But I'm his mommy. I want to raise him with enough security and courage to find his way in life. I would do anything in the world to protect him from earthly harm, but what if there were something ahead for him that I couldn't do anything about and that God could but he didn't? How would I handle that? I have no idea. I still fight with the old "God wants us to jump through hoops to prove our devotion to him" mentality, as if God rips out our heart to test our loyalty. In my spirit I don't believe

God is like this, but in my mind, and in the darker history book of my life, I still hear those relentless fears.

That's why I'm writing this book—not because I get it all, but because I want to learn. I want to trust God enough to look directly into his face and say yes, without fear or resignation, to all he has for me.

MISSING THE POINT

"I am still confident of this: I will see the goodness of the LORD in the land of the living" (Psalm 27:13).

That's quite a verse. I used to read it as I lay on the floor of my room in the hospital. I couldn't believe it was true. In the land of the living! Right here . . . right now! I'm always missing the point with God, deaf to his outrageous punch line.

I'm like William, my father-in-law. We sat by the fire one Christmas Eve playing Scattergories. If you know the game, you're up to speed. If not, here it is in a nutshell: Each player has a card with the same list of items, such as, "A Boy's Name," "U.S. Cities," "Things That Are Cold," ya da, ya da, ya da . . . you get the idea. Someone spins a wheel, and it stops on a letter. Each player quickly fills out the list with answers that begin with the same letter. (There is a time limit.) The letter that evening was "P." One of the items was "Musical Groups." I wrote "Point of Grace." Barry wrote "the Pointer Sisters." William wrote . . . "the Lennon Sisters."

I said to him, "Pop, the Lennon Sisters begins with 'L.'"

"So, can I use it?" William asked.

"No. It's supposed to be a group beginning with 'P.' There is no 'P' in the Lennon Sisters. Not anywhere. 'P' is not present. There is a total lack of 'P.'"

He thought for a few moments. "So, can I use it?"

Good grief! Oh, why not. Yes, you can use it!

Missed the point!

So it is in our relationship with God. We miss the point.

My mother-in-law got the point in a startling way. In May of 1999, we buried Eleanor Pfaehler after nursing her through the final stages of liver cancer. I watched a strong, redheaded, feisty, sixty-six-year-old woman become a child again, ravaged by cancer, reduced to a shadow. But I saw something else as well—something I didn't even want to see at first, but something that was so present it would have been like trying to pretend there wasn't a water buffalo in your bath when there clearly was. I saw Eleanor find in her dying what she had been looking for in her living. She was at peace. She wrapped her heart around God's will and said Yes! She let go of control.

I never thought I'd see her let go. She could match me, trench for trench, fists ready, any day of the week. I had prayed so often for paths into her life and heart. It was as if I asked too much. Barry is an only child. William and Eleanor waited twelve years after their wedding to have him and then, when we married, she felt she was losing him to another woman. Eleanor and I fought quiet battles. We both tried in our flawed sinful states to love better, but we were constantly defeated.

I remember so many silly things we did in our battle of the wills. She and William would stay with us for a few weeks at a time. I would go out for an hour or so on an errand, and when I returned I would discover that she moved one of my lamps to a different table. I'd wait until she went to bed, then I'd move it back. She said they always had ham at Thanksgiving; I said we always had turkey. She bought a big ham, and I bought a big turkey; on Thanksgiving the four of us stared at enough food to sink a ship.

She had a lot of health problems apart from her cancer. I would ask her every day how she was feeling. Then I got sick with a severe case of bronchitis while she was visiting, and she never asked me how I felt. It wasn't like I was dying, but I wanted her to care about me and I didn't think she did. We constantly failed to connect with each other. If I sat with the whole family for a long time around the breakfast table, she said I never gave her any time alone with Barry. If I went off for a couple of hours to give them some time, she asked Barry why I was avoiding her.

Our last Christmas together was terrible. Eleanor was dying, and she knew it. She knew it would be her last Christmas, and she wanted us to hear and respond to her silent pleas. She needed us to ignore what was actually coming out of her mouth and hear her deeper cry to be loved. But I was very deaf that month. All I could hear was that she wouldn't talk to me or that what she said was unkind.

"Would you like to go for a ride in the car?" I asked.

"No."

"Then I think I might."

"Fine, just do what makes you happy," she replied, with an edge to her voice that cut through the air like a frozen sword.

"Can I get you anything?"

Silence.

"Mom?"

Silence.

I wanted it to be Eleanor's best Christmas ever, and since I'm a Christmas girl, I just knew I could make this one wonderful for her. I remembered from visits to Charleston that she liked to decorate to the hilt. So I had wreaths on every window. I had a huge one covered with fruit on the front door. There were angels galore hanging from everything that wasn't moving. It was a veritable winter wonderland. But Eleanor would hardly come out of her room.

One evening as I was rocking Christian to sleep, I heard raised voices in the kitchen. Eleanor and Barry were having a blazing row. Later that night I managed to squeeze out of Barry that his mom felt I had pushed her out of his life. Barry was angry. Eleanor was angry. And I was angry. For two days she wouldn't talk to me at all. As she pushed me away, I fell into my familiar trap of thinking that life is all about me—and I just gave up. I stopped trying to get through to her.

But God had different plans. In the weeks before Eleanor died, God answered our prayers with a generosity that silenced us. We sat together holding hands. As I bathed her, rubbed her feet, changed her diaper, and sang to her, we found ourselves at the throne of grace. I remember one evening when I thought she was asleep. I held her hand and began to sing "Great Is Thy Faithfulness." Suddenly she joined in. Her throat was parched; it was hard for her to swallow, but she sang out exactly what she was living in: In the worst days of her life, she was bathed in the faithfulness of God.

After that night we had many midnight conversations that deeply influenced my whole life, not just my relationship with my mother-in-law. I remember very well one of those conversations. Eleanor had just sipped a little ginger ale, which soothed her dry mouth and throat. I was sitting alongside the hospital bed in her bedroom, with the rail down so we could be closer. I was rubbing cream into her hands when she stopped me and put her hand on my face, the way I do with Christian.

"I never meant those things I said at Christmas, Sheila."

"I know, Mom."

"No, please let me say this. I was just so afraid. I felt so alone. I looked at you and William and Barry and Christian, and I knew I'd be gone soon, and you'd all go on without me. I knew I'd never see Christian on his first day of school or on the day of his first prom. When I'm scared, I get mean. I'm sorry."

Me too, I thought.

"But I'm not afraid anymore," she said. "I've never been so at peace in my life."

Tears rolled down both of our cheeks. I laid my head on the pillow next to hers for a long time.

Being there has changed me. I'll never be the same again. I saw a woman who had made herself miser-

> *I felt as if I was on holy ground. I saw a look on her face I'd never seen before—and it was beautiful.*

able for most of her life trying to feel wanted and loved finally find it on the final few steps home. I saw that you can spend your whole life grabbing control and never be free—or you can, like Eleanor in those precious last few days, say yes to God without fear, let go into his arms of love, and be set free—finally free. What I saw in Eleanor's eyes was not the yes of defeated resignation; it was the yes of finally "getting it" that God is good.

Eleanor did not want to die. She wasn't old, according to today's standards of "oldness." She had a lot to live for. But when it finally became clear to her that she was going to die, she said Yes! The fear was gone; joy and peace were in its place. I don't pretend to understand it all. I was there with her, but she was in Christ's arms, enfolded in a special grace that left me speechless. I felt as if I was on holy ground. I saw a look on her face I'd never seen before—and it was beautiful.

This look reflects the divine paradox that it is only in *giving up control* of our lives that we ever will be free. Cancer took fifty pounds from Eleanor's frame; it took her liver and battered it to a pulp. But God stretched her soul, lifted her spirit, and carried her home singing all the way. She had shouted most of her life. Her final whispered words were honest and kind and true, and they rang loudly with faith.

Between No and Yes

When I look closely at what Dag Hammarskjöld wrote ("For all that has been—Thanks! For all that shall be—Yes!"), there is more there than I can wrap my heart around. I believe he is saying that for every single thing that has happened in our lives, we can learn to say with confidence, even with joy, "Not my will, but yours be done." This means saying yes to the happy and beautiful gifts, but also to the child you lost, the husband who never showed up, the breast cancer, the lost opportunities, the broken dreams, the endless list of human suffering. I certainly don't believe he is suggesting that all the pain in our lives is inflicted by God to see if he can squeeze a heartbroken yes out of us. But I do embrace the mystery that, in the darkest valleys, even when saying yes will break our hearts, the Light of the world is with us, and we will come to know him, to love and trust him, in ways we never have before.

I think back to a conversation I had with a woman in Phoenix, Arizona, at a Women of Faith conference. I had been signing books and listening to a patchwork quilt of stories for about an hour. I saw her out of the corner of my eye. She was standing off to one side. She looked fragile, uncertain, alone. I smiled at her and signaled that as soon as I could I would come over to where she was. She smiled back. When the crowd thinned out, I joined her. We talked for a few moments about the events of the evening. I could tell she was carefully circling her story, searching for the internal strength to put words to the unspeakable.

"I came to Christ as a result of the death of my child," she said with tears spilling onto thin, pale cheeks.

She must have recognized the uncertainty in my eyes, and she continued to place pieces in the painful puzzle of her life story.

"I wasn't a believer when my son was born. I guess I was an agnostic. I never gave God much thought. Then he got really sick."

"What was wrong with him?" I asked.

"Oh, it was a very rare disease. It took me a few weeks just to be able to spell it! It was a blood disorder. They told me he wouldn't make it to his first birthday, but he did. He lived to be almost three years old."

I thought back to earlier that evening. I thought of Christian, my three-year-old, who came bounding onstage, full of life and mischief, intent on carrying out Barbara Johnson's suggestion to stick gum on my nose. I ducked, he laughed, and thousands of women laughed—but did she? Was the sight of my boy too painful a reminder of what she had been robbed of? She continued her story.

"As he got weaker and weaker I felt so helpless. There was nothing I could do. I began to pray; I began to read the Bible."

"Was your prayer that God would heal him?" I asked softly.

"That was part of it. Mostly, I just asked him to help us. When I finally handed my son to Christ, I handed all of me, too."

I had no words. For her, saying yes has left her with an open wound for the rest of her life. But she walks with it; she works with it. She is changed by it. I am aware again that there are those in my life who understand things I don't. Honestly, if losing your child is the price you pay for greater understanding, in all the honesty of my feeble humanity, I'd rather not gain it.

I think back to my experience in the hospital. I don't begin to compare a battle with clinical depression to the loss of a baby, but this mom's pain and grace reminded me of a conversation I had with a friend a year after I was released from the psychiatric unit.

"You are so different, Sheila," she said. "You seem so free."

"That's how I feel," I said. "It's as if God has given me a new life."

"I'm happy for you," she said. "But if that's the only way to get it, I'll pass!"

I smiled and hugged her. I knew exactly what she meant. I would not have chosen this path, but I cannot deny that walking it has changed me profoundly. There is something wonderful here, the edges of which I am still just scarcely scratching. There is a whole way of living that is so freeing, but I am still standing on the edge barely glimpsing it. I think I want to totally abandon myself to God, to take that leap of faith, but I'm still standing. Perhaps you are too.

So why is it so hard for us to give an unreserved yes to God? I have a few guesses:

- We have a bruised picture of love.
- We operate out of fear rather than out of love.
- We feel we are victims of the whims of people and God alike.
- We are afraid God will treat us like trained animals jumping through hoops to entertain a bored deity.
- We don't know what we are saying yes to.

I'm sure you can come up with your own list of reasons why you are holding back. For me, the reasons feel deep and primal. My fear goes back further than I can recall—a weighty cold dread that tells me life is not safe. It warns that if I don't look after myself, who will? If I don't say no, someone—or worse still, God himself—will make me do something I don't want to do, all for the sake of the kingdom. And if it's for the kingdom, it would seem petty to refuse!

But saying no is suffocating me. I'm discovering the difference between living at peace and grasping control. I feel the difference between trust and fear. I live with a restless feeling that I'm settling for far less than what God wants for me.

It's like watching Christian with one of his gifts last Christmas. He held the box for the longest time, but he wouldn't open it because it was making a funny noise. Each time I picked it up and offered to open it for him he said, "No"—and made me put it down again. If I put it away in a closet, he made me bring it back out. Finally, when he wasn't looking, I took it into the kitchen and unwrapped the talking Barney he had asked for. He was over the moon when I gave it to him, but he wouldn't have risked opening the gift himself.

That's how I am. I skirt saying yes, but I don't want the package God is offering me out of my sight, because I have a feeling that what I've wanted all my life is in that very package.

One of the most precious gifts I've ever received was given to me by my mother-in-law just before she died. When Barry was growing up, Eleanor would tell him at regular intervals that he shouldn't trust anyone. Even within the extended family there was a tight lock between Barry and his parents. It became an unspoken code (which I was aware of before I joined the family). Eleanor even wanted Barry to get something in writing before he gave me my engagement ring to protect him in case I dumped him and kept the ring. "You can't trust anyone," she reminded him. Barry told her he wouldn't do that. This mistrust was there between Eleanor and me almost until the very end.

Just before she died I asked her how she wanted things to be for the viewing and the funeral. Her face lit up as we sat for a long time, talking everything through in great detail. I wrote it all down so I wouldn't forget a thing. At the most vulnerable moment of her life, Eleanor—the woman who wouldn't trust anyone—entrusted herself to me. The night after she died, Barry, William, and I sat around the table, and I realized I was the only one who knew everything she wanted. What a gift! What a miracle! What a transformation!

It brings me back to Psalm 27, words I read often to Eleanor during her last days:

> The LORD is my light and my salvation—
> whom shall I fear?
> The LORD is the stronghold of my life—
> of whom shall I be afraid?

To take comfort in these words I have to trust the Lord—or they are meaningless. But if, like David, I can find myself on my knees with these words on my lips, I will also say with him:

> I am still confident of this:
> I will see the goodness of the LORD
> in the land of the living.
> Wait for the LORD;
> be strong and take heart
> and wait for the LORD.

To see God's goodness in the land of the living seemed too good to be true not so long ago. I'm beginning, just beginning, to get it. I'm discovering that the first step toward this kind of vital, trusting relationship with God is *speaking the truth*—bringing myself out of the shadows and talking honestly to my Father. I know now that it's all right to be afraid.

A Fearful Prayer

Dear God,

I would find it much easier to follow you if you would just let me look at the map. I don't like surprises. They bring out in me what is not always very attractive. I feel threatened, vulnerable. I hate that. Sometimes I'm scared of you, Lord, as if you have all these "surprises" ahead and I won't be prepared. Maybe I won't like the surprises at all. Can't we do this "life" thing together and both have input? . . . You don't have to answer that.

Sheila

2

THIS IS NOT WHAT
I HAD PLANNED

*If God would only use his fingers and make us broken bread and
poured-out-wine in a special way! But when he uses someone whom
we dislike, or some set of circumstances to which we said we would
never submit, and makes those the crushers, we object. We must
never try to choose the scene of our own martyrdom.*

Oswald Chambers

*"I tell you the truth, unless a kernel of wheat falls to the ground and
dies, it remains only a single seed. But if it dies, it produces many seeds."*
Jesus Christ—John 12:24

Whatever, Lord!

Barbara Johnson

Where are you taking me?

"Stand here, Mommy," Christian said, pointing to a spot
on our front lawn, a less-than-innocent grin on his
face.

Not that old trick again!

"Not a chance, buddy," I replied.

"Oh, pleeeeeeeease, Mommy. Just stand here. It'll be fine,
really. Pleeeeeeease!"

I looked at my clothes. They were just back from the dry
cleaners. I thought about my hair. Today I had actually dried
it as opposed to the usual stick-a-baseball-cap-on-it approach
I reserve for home.

Then I looked at my boy's face. His brown eyes were dancing with mischief as he hopped from foot to foot, hoping he could pull off this trick on his mommy just one more time.

So ... I stood there. Out came the garden hose from behind his back, and a moment later I was soaked to the skin.

I knew exactly what was going to happen. It happened last time and the time before that. His "Just stand here. It'll be fine, really" fell on well-informed ears. Soggy, well-informed ears.

Perhaps that's why it's hard for us to give an unreserved yes to God. We know what's coming down the pipeline. We've said yes before, and we got soaked to the skin. But it's been a lot more painful than being blasted in the face with the shock of the spray of cold water from a dancing boy. It's left us breathless. For most of us, it started a long time ago. It did for me.

I've spent much of my life afraid of men, especially strong men. I was comfortable around those who were easily impressed, nondemanding, or so badly wounded themselves that they seemed no threat to me. But strong, confident men unsettled me. I didn't know how to behave around them.

As I look through old family photos now, I understand. I started off well. Many of us do. If we are blessed by being born into a family where our arrival is eagerly anticipated, we're off to a great start. Christian's comment to me the other evening reminded me of this. Barry, William, and I sat with him to read a story before he went to bed. He put the book down, looked at all of us, and proclaimed, "This is cool! We are a family." You could have cooked hot dogs over the glow on his face.

Very young children naturally trust. But my father's illness and subsequent death repainted my own internal pictures of love, safety, and trust. Because of his mental illness before he died, my dad gave the impression that he hated me. I sewed that new picture into my soul in words a mile high: *No one loves you forever; no one is completely safe.* So, even when I gave my life to God as an eleven-year-old, I did so through this paradigm of

> *No one loves you forever; no one is completely safe.*

conditions. I wanted to say yes to him, but I was afraid of what he would ask of me, and I was convinced that it would hurt. So I couldn't say yes; I couldn't say no. I couldn't even whisper what I felt. It would have made it too real. But, even as a child, I knew that this was where I wanted to live my life—under the wings of God. So I crawled under and tried to find a safe spot:

> He who dwells in the shelter of the Most High
> > will rest in the shadow of the Almighty.
> I will say of the LORD, "He is my refuge and my fortress,
> > my God, in whom I trust."
> Surely he will save you from the fowler's snare
> > and from the deadly pestilence.
> He will cover you with his feathers,
> > and under his wings you will find refuge;
> > his faithfulness will be your shield and rampart.
> > > *Psalm 91:1*

This was my favorite psalm. I wanted to believe it was true, but under the comfort of these words lay the reality of my young life. My dad was a good man. He was a man who loved God. Yet he had seemed to grow to hate me. And now he was gone.

While I love to sort through old family photographs because of the sense of belonging and roots they give me, I find some of them awfully hard to look at. Take, for example, the one taken in the backyard of the home in which I was born. I'm about three. My sister, Frances, and I are standing on either side of a chair. My dad is in the chair. He tries to smile, but a stroke had left half of his face paralyzed, and so the smile comes out funny and crooked, like he's doing a bad Jimmy Cagney impersonation. It makes me really sad to look at this photograph. Perhaps that's why we sometimes find it so hard to say yes to God. Old memories remind us of painful things that have led us to believe it's not safe to totally trust anyone—not even God.

My own child trusts me, even when he is afraid. Once I took him to Seuss Landing at Universal Studios Escape in Florida. He wanted to go on "The Cat in the Hat" ride. I looked at the sign for some indication as to what the ride was like; the sign said it was appropriate for any child who could walk. Christian was two-and-a-half years old, so we got on. But the minute the car began to spin around he screamed out, "Mommy, I'm afraid. I want off!" I told him I was so sorry he was afraid, but we couldn't get off until the ride stopped. So he said, "Okay, then hold my hand."

This was a profound moment for me. I'm the one who took him on the dumb ride, and yet he wanted to hold *my* hand. So unlike me! If someone hurts me or does something that makes me afraid, I want to push them away. The thought would never cross my mind to run to them or ask them to hold my hand. Christian feels no need at this point in his life to protect himself from me. I'm there for him. I'm his mommy. That's how it should be, and that's how I started off too. So why do we change?

Adult choices can decimate children. The tragedies of life can pull the rug right out from under their safe, trusting feet. Children don't understand death or divorce or parental absence or neglect. They think they must have contributed in some way to ruin this perfect picture of *family*. At a gut level, what they experience is that nothing is safe anymore. They can't count on anything being forever or being ultimately for their good.

Perhaps you felt unloved as a child. Perhaps your father didn't die; he just left one day and never came home. Or your mom was there, but she wasn't there. You stood in the background of her life, jumping up and down, crying out, Can't you see me, Mommy? I'm right here!

This emotional loss may be even harder than losing a parent to death. You have to live with the awareness that your dad or mom could have been with you and chose not to be. We all carry scars into the courts of heaven, and the yes we want to give to God carries a lot of reservations because of who we are and where we've been and what we believe at the very core of our lives. Can we really trust God's direction day by day when some of the paths we've already walked have been strewn with sorrows?

GOD'S PLANS

I love my friend Luci Swindoll's sense of humor. It's witty and full of the pure joy of being alive. Among the things she hates most are legalism and control, because they squeeze the life out of joy.

Luci recently asked the audience at a Women of Faith conference what God and the control freak have in common. Answer: "They both love you and have a wonderful plan for your life." We all laughed heartily, but it's the truth. We're all acquainted with someone who thinks they know what we should be doing.

Perhaps this is our problem with God as well. He is known for his plans. You know the verse; it's got to be one of the most frequently quoted verses in the Bible: "'For I know the plans I have for you,' declares the LORD, 'plans to prosper you and not to harm you, plans to give you hope and a future'" (Jeremiah 29:11).

Well, wait just a moment before you take up an offering in the warm glow of this comforting promise. What if I have a different plan? What if my hopes and dreams are different from God's? I agree it could be quite a ride to say yes to God, but I'd like to know where we're going, please. I'm open to a lot of places, but there *are* a few destinations on my blacklist.

These fearful destinations are not just on my list; they're probably on yours as well. Most of us share two great fears in particular:

1. Losing what we have or love.
2. Never receiving what we want most.

At a Women of Faith conference in August of 1999, I talked to a German girl who was backpacking across the United States.

"I don't like what you said tonight," she told me. "You said that Eleanor, your mother-in-law, was in a better place when she died."

"That's right," I said. "She found the peace and rest she'd been looking for all her life."

"But why didn't God heal her?"

"I don't know. There are some things I'll never understand this side of heaven."

"I don't like a God like that."

As she walked off, I noticed that she had bought three of my books. *Dear God, let the wrestling match begin,* I prayed.

> *What if my hopes and dreams are different from God's?*

On another occasion I talked with a young woman at the end of a conference in San Diego. "I want to give everything to God," she told me, "but I'm so afraid he'll take away my boyfriend or make me change careers or do something I'll hate."

Her fears seemed reasonable to me. Perhaps her boyfriend wasn't a Christian. Perhaps God *would* choose a different path for her life. I didn't know what to say that would make her feel any better. She wanted something in writing from God, guaranteeing that if she said yes to him, it wouldn't change the path of her own chosen destiny. But God has written all he will write, and no such promise exists.

This is one of the greatest deterrents to an unconditional yes to God, isn't it? He might take away what we love or fail to give us what we want.

I talked to still another woman in the summer of 1999 whose pain was so close to the surface it was agonizing to watch. Her husband had died three months before of brain cancer.

"I feel like raw clay," she said. "I'm sure God is going to make something new with me, with this broken vessel of my life, but I don't know if I'm ready for it. I don't think I even want to know what it is. I know God is with me on this trip, but I have no idea where he's taking me. All I know is that the husband I loved is gone."

I hugged her, and my heart ached as I watched her walk away.

When Christian was a few days old, he ended up in pediatric intensive care for a night. It was a very scary time. As it turned out, it was a technician's mistake; we took him home the next morning, but it made for an interesting night. The whole pediatric unit was a model of the best care a child could receive. Christian looked ridiculously healthy compared to some of the tiny premature babies fighting for their lives in Plexiglas boxes. One woman was holding her three-pound baby to her chest, whispering "No! No! No!" I have wondered since if she too was in a wrestling match with God, afraid he was asking her to relinquish her child, fighting that thought tooth and nail.

I look at that great verse in Jeremiah again, "'For I know the plans I have for you,' declares the LORD, 'plans to prosper you . . .'" But what if we don't like God's plan? What if our own plans for the future clash with his? And what exactly does God mean by "prosper," anyway? I've talked to people who are trying desperately to bargain with God over a heartfelt desire. "I'll do anything if you heal him, God; just don't take him." "Please, Lord, if you'll just give me this job, this house, this mate, then I'll do anything you ask." What they are terrified to pray is, "Lord, have your way," because God's way might be different from theirs. It might be the very thing they dread.

THE FEAR OF LOSS

For years I have wrestled with Jesus' words about his own death: "I tell you the truth, unless a kernel of wheat falls to the ground and dies, it remains only a single seed. But if it dies, it produces many seeds" (John 12:24). It's clear in this context that his death in our place gave spiritual life—a rebirth—to millions who put their faith in him. But what of us? Does it mean that we have to let go of our own dreams in order to receive God's greater harvest?

I know that when I left *The 700 Club*, I unwrapped this verse in a very personal way. I remember driving out of the gates of The Christian Broadcasting Network, wondering if my ministry was over. There is such a stigma in our nation, and particularly in the church, about mental illness. I was pretty sure that, once people knew I'd been hospitalized for clinical depression, I would be ostracized. But I'd come to the place in my life where this fear could not stop me from getting well and growing in my relationship with God. I felt like such a phony, smiling on the outside and miserable on the inside. All I knew was that I wanted to "get real." I wanted to *truly* find God in the midst of my "religious" life. It's amazing how easy it is to lose God in the midst of the trappings of our faith. I had no peace. I was full of fear. I remember thinking,

If this career of mine is something I've been propping up, then it should die. I'm not going to try for one moment to salvage anything. I'm going to walk away and let this seed fall and die.

I knew that if I wanted to develop a truly intimate, honest, and liberating relationship with God, I was going to have to unclench my fists and let go of all the things I was clinging to for dear life. There was no room in this relationship for all my excess baggage. Fear had to go. Pride had to go. Control had to go. I just had no idea what would fill the hole their departure would leave in my soul.

It was, and continues to be, a long journey. What I didn't know then was that there were five other women on this path who were going to become part of my family. I never for a moment thought that God would place me on a ministry team of some of the best women I've ever met in my life. If I hadn't let go of my baggage, I'd have been left at the gate.

I consider it one of the greatest privileges of my life to be part of the Women of Faith team. As we travel around the country one of the hallmarks of our conferences is that we tell the truth. This might sound like a strange thing to say about a Christian event. Don't we always tell the truth? I don't think so. Most of us tell what we wish were true. We tell who we wish we were. We feel it would somehow diminish God if we are not "up to par," shining lights in his constellation. But this lack of transparency separates those who wish to minister from those who want to be helped and encouraged. As if we aren't all in the same boat.

So I'll lay my fears out on the table. Perhaps they are yours too.

My worst fear is that something will happen to my son, to my darling Christian. I was forty when I got pregnant. I had given up hope of ever being a mommy. For most of my pregnancy we thought there was something wrong with our baby.

After eight months of my doctor reading the wrong woman's chart, mistakenly placed into my file, the wonder of this child, when he arrived, was even greater. On December 13, 1996, out popped this perfect boy.

I remember the first time I looked at him. He was wet and slippery and crying and very cross. I was sore and tired and giddy. But I'd never seen a more beautiful sight. Barry and I cried right along with Christian. It's become a family trait! Now, as I stand by my table at Women of Faith conferences and hear stories of parents who have lost a child, I think I couldn't bear it.

Whenever I get back to the hotel after another conference has come to an end, I hug my boy. He's often fast asleep in our king-size bed. We send Sarah, Christian's nanny and play-mate, off to her room, and Barry and I crawl in beside our boy. He doesn't really wake up, but he senses that I'm there. I feel his little hands twist a piece of my hair and his feet tuck under my knees, and as I hold him, I lift up to the Lamb of God all the people who have shared their stories with me.

Let me say again, I know that Christian doesn't belong to me, but I'm his mommy. I'm not just afraid something will happen to him; I'm afraid something will happen to me. I've never had this feeling before becoming a mom. I always rested secure in the knowledge that my life is in God's hands, and that if I died, I would be home. While I know this is still true, I feel very differently now. If my son falls and hurts himself, if he's afraid, he calls for me. My little boy needs his mom, and I want to be there. I'm also afraid something will happen to Barry. I watched my brother, Stephen, grow up without a dad, and it's not a good thing for a boy. A boy needs his father. Occasionally I'll see a talk show where teenage girls talk about wanting to become mothers, and I think, *You don't have a clue what this is about. It's not about you. It's about that precious life. Buy a dog! Get a fish!*

I don't walk around every day nursing my horrors. I keep them in their own room. But Eleanor's death brought my fears into sharp focus. I had nightmares for several days after Eleanor's funeral. These bad dreams were all about being out of control. I felt as though I were falling into a hole. Then, when we were flying to Detroit for a conference, Christian was asleep in my lap, and I found myself checking to see if he was still breathing. Some time has passed now, and I'm doing much better, but I still feel vulnerable. All of my fears fall into the areas where I have no control.

Surely this is the most primal fear of all— that we will end up all alone.

I feel a need to understand if I'm alone in this. I asked my friend, Patsy Clairmont, what she is afraid of. Her answer made me weep.

"It's twofold," she said. "One fear would be losing Les [her husband of thirty-eight years who is struggling with severe diabetes]. We've been together since I was seventeen. He is part of my cells, the filter through which I breathe and see my life. Another would be that he would lose a limb. He's always been such an active man. I don't know what that would do to his spirit."

Very real, tangible fears. No control.

I asked Barry what he is afraid of. He is afraid of cancer. It runs in his family, and he wonders if it's in him. Two of his mom's sisters live with cancer, and he watched it ravage his mother. No control.

I asked the same question of Pat Wenger, traveling companion of my Women of Faith colleague Marilyn Meberg. Her answer cut through all the surface fears. "Abandonment," she said. Surely this is the most primal fear of all—that we will end up all alone. No control. Jealousy, anger, controlling behavior—all have their roots in our fear of being abandoned.

I talk to hundreds of people when I speak at conferences. I read the mail they send me. Their fears fall into these painfully familiar holes: losing something/someone they have; not getting something/someone they want.

In *Mere Christianity*, C. S. Lewis quotes a schoolboy who was asked what God is like. The boy replied, "The sort of person who is always snooping around to see if anyone is enjoying himself, and then trying to stop it." A funny answer, perhaps, but at some core level many of us share this fear. We think, *This is too good. Life is too smooth. God is going to throw a wrench in the works at any moment.* Perhaps this is why Paul urged the members of the church in Philippi to "continue to work out [their] salvation with fear and trembling" (Philippians 2:12). It's a scary business to trust God with total abandon. "Fear and trembling" are not popular words. I'd much rather have joy and hope. Or laughter and mercy. But fear and trembling? Not good PR words.

I joined the Women of Faith team in February of 1997, when Christian was just six weeks old. I knew Barbara Johnson's story because I'd interviewed her on *The 700 Club*. But I had become a mommy since then. As I sat onstage for the first time and heard her enumerate the tragedies that had decimated her life, I was horrified. I was the new kid on the block, so I had to behave and look borderline sane, but I could have laid on the floor of the arena and sobbed.

Barbara talked about her husband, Bill, and his car accident. He wasn't expected to live. He'd sustained a severe brain injury, which had left him blind. But God has healed him. As Bill walked onstage to say hello, we all cheered and whistled.

Then Barb moved on to the death of her son Steven. He had been killed in Vietnam, and because of Bill's condition at the time, she had to go identify the body by herself. I tried to control myself, but I felt as if someone had grabbed hold of my heart with an iron fist and was squeezing the life out of it. I felt sick.

Then she told us about the car wreck that took the life of her son Tim. It was five years to the day when she went once again to identify the body of one of her boys in a funeral home. Bill could have gone this time, but she wanted to spare him the nightmare picture that was etched into her mind and heart from identifying Steven the first time around. It was unspeakable.

"You really need the grace of God when you stand and look at what's left of your firstborn son, delivered from Canada in pieces in an orange crate," she said.

I sat with my head in my hands and sobbed. The thought of this ever happening to my little boy was more than I could bear.

Barbara kept on going. When her third son became estranged from the family, disappearing into the homosexual subculture for eleven years, Barb contemplated taking her life. But then she said something that surprised me. Finally, she said, after a year of grief so intense she could barely function, she prayed what she calls the prayer of relinquishment: "Whatever, Lord! Whatever you bring into my life, it's all right. Like Job said, 'Though he slay me, yet will I hope in him'" (Job 13:15).

Everyone applauded this great statement of surrender from this remarkable woman whom I have come to love like I love my own mother. But I wanted to run off the stage, out of the building, and off the team. It was too much for me. All my worst fears came rushing to the surface.

Is God going to do that to me so that I can have a great, victorious story to tell from the stage? I wondered in horror. *If so, I'm going to get a job at Wal-Mart.* And I really meant it. All right, perhaps Nordstrom.

I talked to Barbara later that day at the hotel and told her how I felt. She said to me, "Sheila, you're trying to put yourself in my shoes but without the grace God gave me, without the huge 'comfort blanket' of love he wrapped me in. When I left the funeral home after identifying Tim's remains, God gave me an incredible gift. I looked up into the sky, and I saw Tim's face smiling down at me. That kind of thing is not in my Baptist background, but I sure needed it. He said, 'Don't cry, Mom, I'm not there. I'm worshiping Jesus around the throne of grace.'"

"I think that's awesome, Barb," I said. "But I want Christian here with me."

"I know," she said, as she gave me a hug. "I wanted Tim too."

As I put Christian to bed that night in our hotel room, I sat beside his crib for a while, watching him as he slept. I wanted to imprint every image of him into my soul. I listened to the little noises he makes with his mouth when he's sleeping. His lips move as if he is planting little kisses on God's cheek. He had a lot of hair for a six-week-old baby, and it curled round his ears. I leaned over and smelled his neck. He smelled like summer.

When Barry fell asleep, I took a bath. As I lay in the tub I poured my heart out to God: *I feel like I'm in a wrestling match here, Lord, and you're bigger. You're going to win. I know you've given everything to me. I know you gave me your own Son, so surely you understand how hard this is. I want to trust you more. I want to. You'll need to teach me how, though, for I don't have a clue.*

I picked up my Bible, which I now keep in the bathroom so I can take advantage of a few quiet moments alone with the Lord, and I read these words: "Are you tired? Worn out?

Burned out on religion? Come to me. On vacation with me, you'll recover your life. I'll show you how to take a real rest. Walk with me and work with me—watch how I do it. Learn the unforced rhythms of grace. I won't lay anything heavy or ill-fitting on you. Keep company with me and you'll learn to live freely and lightly" (Matthew 11:28–29, THE MESSAGE).

"Thank you, Lord," I whispered, tears streaming down my face. I climbed out of the tub and went to sleep.

THE FEAR OF SHATTERED DREAMS

Our other great fear is that we will not get what we want most. We fear that our vision for our life will remain just that—a vision, never a reality. What if our greatest dream is to be married and to have a child, and it never happens? What if we live with chronic pain and all we want is a pain-free week? What if we have a clear picture in our minds of what success in our career would look like, but God seems to be withholding our dreams?

- Why don't you do things that you *could* do, Lord?
- How would it hurt you to give me a husband?
- Why do you give babies to thirteen-year-old guests on the Jerry Springer show while I sit here with empty arms?
- Why do other people achieve their goals while mine always seem just beyond my reach?
- When will the pain stop? You are all-powerful. Why won't you give me some relief?

I went with Sarah, Christian's nanny, to a movie recently. As we walked across the parking lot, I asked her, "What's your greatest fear?"

"That I'll never find my real purpose in life," she answered. "That I'll live my whole life and not quite get what it was all about. If God showed up in front of me and said, 'No husband, no children, no big career, Sarah. That's my plan, and it's good,' I think I'd be fine with that. It's just not knowing what I really should be doing with my life that's so scary."

> *Things rarely turn out exactly as we plan them.*

I understand. I once talked to a Catholic priest at a monastery in California. I had gone there as part of a Spiritual Disciplines course I was taking at Fuller Theological Seminary. We were talking about the fear we have that perhaps we've misread God and said yes to something he never asked of us.

"Wouldn't it be funny," he said, "if when every priest gets to heaven God says, 'You misunderstood me. I said "Celebrate!" not "Celibate!"'"

When she speaks to audiences, Luci Swindoll often says that life is disappointing. It never quite measures up to the fruit of a fertile imagination. She's right. You really can't argue with it. Things rarely turn out exactly as we plan them.

When Barry and I were married, he had no idea that I had such a thing about cats and dogs. We'd been married about two weeks when it raised its furry head. He was at work, and I was taking the garbage outside. It had snowed, and it was bitterly cold. I saw a dog sitting on my doormat when I got back from the dumpster. It had no collar on, and it was shivering. I knocked on our neighbor's door and asked her if she knew where this dog belonged. She said she thought it was a stray. Of course I took it in. I gave it a bowl of soup, wrapped it in a blanket, and set it by the fire.

This is cool! I thought. *We have a dog!*

I called Barry at work. "We have a dog!" I said.

"What! What do you mean we have a dog? We live in an apartment. We can't have a dog!" he bellowed.

"It's just a wee little dog," I reasoned. "I want to keep it."

"We can't keep it, Babe, I'm sorry."

"Just wait till you see it," I pleaded. "You'll love it."

Barry opened the front door that evening and asked, "Well, where is this dog?"

"He's right over ... oh, no!"

I looked on in horror as the dog relieved itself on Barry's favorite blue silk sofa. My husband called the Humane Society, and my doggy was gone.

A few days later I saw an ad in the paper for Russian Blue kittens. *That would be cool*, I thought. I called the number, and the man who was the breeder ran the Jim Reeves Museum in Nashville. I took this as a sign from God, because Jim Reeves was a Christian. I got in the car.

I've never seen so many cats in my life. The hut in which they lived stunk. *But just one cat won't stink*, I thought. I picked out a kitten and took it home in a box. I decided to hide the kitten in the bathroom till I could evaluate Barry's mood when he came home. I made his favorite meal, changed into a nice outfit, and put on makeup.

He was in a great mood. We ate and talked, and then I said, "How would you like a Christian cat?"

"What on earth is a Christian cat, and no, I wouldn't!" he replied.

"Oh," I said.

"Sheila! What have you done?"

"Nothing much, but there's a kitten in the bathroom singing 'The Old Rugged Cross.'"

He looked at me as if I needed to be back in the psych ward.

"Come and take a look," I said.

I opened the bathroom door and couldn't believe what I saw. There were great wads of black gook all over the walls.

"What's this?" Barry asked—and before the words were out of his mouth, the kitten shook its head again and out shot some more gook from its ears. The kitten went back. Sorry, Jim!

In the spring I decided to swing by the Humane Society and just visit their dogs and cats. The front room contained cage after cage of every kind of cat imaginable. One cat was wrapped in bandages.

"What's wrong with this cat?" I asked.

"It was looking for a warm place to sleep," the attendant told me. "Unfortunately, it crawled up into a car engine, and when the driver started his car, it ripped its back open."

I thought of the hymn "Rescue the Perishing," and I took the cat home. When I got to the house, I wrote Barry a note:

Dear Barry,

I have rescued a cat with no back. Well, it has no fur on its back, and it has thirty-three stitches. His name is Max. I'm going to care for him at least until he is well. I will call you after you get home and read this note, and you can let me know if Max and I can come home. If not, you may visit us at the YWCA.

Your loving wife,
Sheila

Max and I got to stay!

There are five more animal stories I won't bore you with here. The point is, Barry married a nut. We are all flawed, and nothing down here on Planet Earth is as perfect as we might imagine. There is no husband or wife in the world who is everything his or her spouse needs or wants. Children grow up and make their own choices—some good and some disastrous. Some men and women wait all their lives for the promotion they deserve, and it never comes. Couples pray month after month for a child, but their arms and hearts remain empty. It is a helpless feeling to live in a world where we have such little control over the events that unfold before us, where we are never sure where God is taking us.

PLAN B

On an early summer evening in 1999 I sat out on the deck of our home in Franklin, Tennessee, under the moonlight, watching the fireflies illumine the night like tiny dancing Chinese lanterns. I was tired. I was overwhelmed by the events of the last few months. We had buried my mother-in-law only a month before. It was hard to believe, but in some ways it seemed much longer ago.

I tried to recall the good moments in Eleanor's final battle. They were few, but highly treasured. I was grateful for the new intimacy we shared as I sat beside her in the upstairs bedroom she and William had shared for all forty-six of their years as husband and wife. We tried to talk her into letting us put the hospital bed from hospice care downstairs. "It would be best for everyone," we said. "No," she said. She wanted to be upstairs surrounded by her vast doll collection.

I recalled the day I was lying on a table in Saint Joseph's Hospital in Orange County, California, and the ultrasound nurse said, "It's a boy!" I remember thinking, "Oh, thank you, Lord!" If it had been a girl, I was doomed to inherit a bazillion dolls, some of which would give me nightmares. There were two in particular that gave me the creeps. They were old store-window mannequins. They stood in the bedroom, propped up against the wall and staring vacantly ahead, faintly menacing, decidedly mothballed.

But on the day we laid Eleanor to rest under an old weeping willow covered in Spanish moss, I told Barry I wanted his mother's doll collection. I wanted to treasure what had mattered to her—and I also wanted to live with the intensity she had died with. There was something mysterious there, something beyond my understanding at the time. In those final days, I witnessed a woman's total surrender. It wasn't defeat; I have seen that. It wasn't despair; I have tasted that. It was a voluntary Yes! to God.

I witnessed a woman's total surrender. It wasn't defeat; I have seen that. It wasn't despair; I have tasted that. It was a voluntary Yes! to God.

Losing Eleanor has made me more vulnerable. I stood beside her casket for the whole two hours of the viewing. I looked calm and together; I looked like the perfect daughter-in-law taking care of things. Yet, inside, I was screaming. I wanted to grab hold of her and hug her and make it all go away. It hit me with an intensity I couldn't understand. In Scotland, where I was raised, when people die, you never see them again. Caskets are always closed. I had never seen a dead body until Eleanor's viewing. She looked like one of her dolls.

She had asked me just before she died if I would go to the funeral home early and make sure her hair and makeup were the way she liked them. I said I would, but I wasn't prepared for it. I had held her hand, brushed her hair, and painted her toenails in the weeks before her death. Now she lay there, cold and still in the dress she wore to our wedding, with the earrings I wore as a bride. I reached out to fix a piece of her hair, and my hand brushed her cheek. It was cold and waxy. I felt as though I had been slapped by the indecency of death.

There is something about the whole process of death that seems so wrong to me. It suddenly became clear to me that this was never God's plan. I was struck again by the fact that this life will always be disappointing. This was *not* the real plan. We live with "Plan B."

I remembered the tears that ran down Eleanor's emaciated cheeks when I told her that Christian, her only grandchild, would never forget her. Good tears and bad tears. Glad for the thought, but not ready to be gone from his life. We humans were made for eternal life, but we tried to grab control in the Garden of Eden, and now we taste fear, sin, death.

As I reflected on the incredible change in my mother-in-law before her death, I wanted to know *why?* Was she so doped up on morphine that we had anesthetized not just the pain in her body but the reality of her dying? I knew the answer, and it was not that. The truth is that Eleanor was apprehended in the midst of her busy, fretful life and sat for quite some time with Christ. She had always found it hard to be still. She had turned worrying into an art form. She admitted to me that she'd fought God for most of her life because she wasn't sure she'd like his plans. Yet in those final days she spent significant time alone with Christ, and that changed everything.

Oswald Chambers once wrote, "Faith never knows where it is being led, but it loves and knows the One who is leading." That's my prayer: to know the One who *is* in control. To trust him. To love him. But because I'm still telling the truth, I have to admit something: He baffles me.

Sometimes it's our experience of God himself that has left us scared. We counted on God to come through for us, and he didn't. At a sad, unspoken level we now believe God is cruel or simply indifferent. What then?

A Fearful Prayer

Dear God,

I find it hard to understand you. If you can stop pain, why don't you? If a child is in a candy store, and you know that she is about to step outside and be hit by a car, why don't you hold her in there a couple more minutes? Send in a cat, or let the store owner offer her a free sucker. No one would know but you. Think of the pain that would be removed from this world if you would just step in. Perhaps you do it all the time. But sometimes, Lord . . . it just doesn't seem enough.

Sheila

3

WHY, WHY, WHY?

A leaking roof can fool the sun, but it cannot fool the rain.

Haitian Proverb

Why is life given to a man
whose way is hidden,
whom God has hedged in?
For sighing comes to me instead of food;
my groans pour out like water.
What I feared has come upon me;
what I dreaded has happened to me.

Job 3:23–25

And now my life ebbs away;
days of suffering grip me.

Job 30:16

If you love me so much, why is life so hard?

It had been six months since my friends, David and Nancy Guthrie, members of our church and our Bible study small group, had buried their baby daughter, Hope. We had Hope's photo in a frame on our Christmas tree. Nancy had made over five hundred of these to give to friends as Christmas gifts. Every time I passed the tree, I looked at Hope's tiny face and thought about Nancy. The Scripture verse they included with the gift was Hebrews 10:23: "Let us hold unswervingly to the hope we profess, for he who promised is faithful."

The first Christmas without their daughter. I couldn't imagine how this would feel. Would they decorate their home, or would they try to forget this Christmas and just focus on making it through the holidays?

Christmas Eve arrived. We decided to go to the five o'clock service at church, because children, even noisy ones, were welcome at that particular service. Christian hadn't been back in "big people's church" since his baptism. (I hoped our pastor had forgotten Christian's public announcement that he was definitely not God.) The church looked beautiful. Candles flickered in every corner.

"Can I blow those out, Mom?"

"Not a chance!"

"Will we sing 'Twinkle, Twinkle Little Star'?"

"Probably not."

The service began, and I was surprised and thrilled as I saw David and Nancy and their son, Matthew, walk onto the platform and sit down on three chairs by a large Christmas tree. Nancy invited all the children to join them for the reading of a story. Christian trotted off down the aisle, the only boy with a ball cap on in church. Nancy read *A Tale of Three Trees*, a traditional American folktale retold by Angela Hunt. It's a wonderful story about what happens to three trees that each have their own special dreams. The first tree wanted to become the most beautiful treasure chest in the world, inlaid with jewels, carrying precious gold. It became the crib that rocked the Christ child. The second tree wanted to be the strongest sailing ship in the world. It became the boat that carried Jesus and his friends through a storm. The third tree never wanted to be cut down. It dreamed of growing to be the tallest tree in the world, a tree so magnificent that those who looked at it would give thanks to God. It became the cross on which Jesus gave his life.

A Tale of Three Trees is a very moving book. It seemed particularly poignant that Nancy had been asked to read that story. Not one of the trees ended up living the life they had imagined. Their dreams were so grand, yet God's plans were greater—even though it meant a surrendering of personal dreams and an experience of such raw pain. One had dreamed of carrying treasure and became instead a humble box—but one that held the Christ child. The second dreamed of being a big, world-renowned sailing ship and became instead a very little boat—but one that became part of a miracle. The third dreamed of all kinds of people looking at it and thanking God because of its powerful appearance—but it never imagined that this dream would be fulfilled in the context of such a blood-soaked event. For David, Nancy, and their son, Matthew, what had they dreamed for this child, this little girl? What did it feel like to trade those dreams for such pain as losing a child? I know they are supposed to feel comforted because God also lost a child—his one and only Son—and he understands their pain, but he could have stopped this—and he didn't. If, having gone through this myself, I would be able to prevent this from ever happening to another family, I would. God did not.

I thought about this as we drove home that evening. That's the rub. It would be like being at the funeral of your child and sitting beside the person who had refused to donate the kidney that might have saved him. You see this mourner cry. You believe he is also brokenhearted, yet he had the power to change the outcome, and he didn't. So, how do you receive comfort from this person? Again I face the brick wall of my humanity, which cannot begin to grasp the ways of God. My only hope is to know the heart of God, and to keep on walking.

Almost six months after Hope's death, Nancy wrote these words in her diary (dated December 3, 1999):

Submission, for me, has meant a quiet, though sorrowful, acceptance of God's plan and God's timing. It meant giving up the plans I had for my daughter, for my family, for my life, and bringing them all under submission to him.

The hardest thing here is that it's not just saying a one-time yes. It's waking up each day and saying yes to God in the midst of the chronic pain of being separated from your daughter.

In *Telling the Truth*, Frederick Buechner reflects on the death of Lazarus, on the grief and sense of betrayal experienced by Lazarus's sisters, Mary and Martha, who were also Jesus' friends. Lazarus had fallen ill, and his sisters had sent word to Jesus, whom they trusted could and would heal their brother. But Jesus did not come. Both Martha and Mary speak poignantly for so many anguished souls when they say, "Lord, if you had been here, my brother would not have died" (John 11:21, 32). Their words are like an accusation: *Why, why, why? Why didn't you come through for us when you could have? What are we supposed to think of you now?*

Buechner zeroes in on Jesus' own tears at Lazarus's tomb, musing that "there seem to have been many levels to his grief":

> It is as if his grief goes so deep that it is for the whole world that Jesus is weeping and the tragedy of the human condition, which is to live in a world where again and again God is not present, at least not in the way and to the degree that man needs him. Jesus sheds his tears at the visible absence of God in the world where the good and bad alike go down to defeat and death. He sheds his tears at the audible silence of God at those moments especially when a word from him would mean the difference between life and death, or at the deafness of men which prevents their hearing him, the blindness of men which prevents even Jesus

himself as a man from seeing him to the extent that at the moment of all moments when he needs him most he cries out his *Eloi, Eloi*, which is a cry so dark that of the four evangelists, only two of them have the stomach to record it as the last word he spoke while he still had a human mouth to speak with. Jesus wept, we all weep, because even when man is good, even when he is Jesus, God makes himself scarce for reasons that no theodicy has ever fathomed.

> *Why must we pay such a high price to glorify our Father?*

Even knowing the happy ending to this story, knowing that Jesus brought Lazarus to life again and glorified his Father through this miracle, I again face the brick wall of my humanity, which cannot begin to grasp the ways of God. *Why must we pay such a high price to glorify our Father?* My only hope is to keep getting to know the heart of God and to keep on walking.

I wonder if this is what Paul was talking about when he implied that the purpose of our lives is to press on through the heartache toward home. Paul spoke as a man who sensed the purpose in all of the pain:

> But whatever was to my profit I now consider loss for the sake of Christ. What is more, I consider everything a loss compared to the surpassing greatness of knowing Christ Jesus my Lord, for whose sake I have lost all things. I consider them rubbish, that I may gain Christ and be found in him, not having a righteousness of my own that comes from the law, but that which is through faith in Christ—the righteousness that comes from God and is by faith.
>
> I want to know Christ and the power of his resurrection and the fellowship of sharing in his sufferings, becoming

like him in his death, and so, somehow, to attain to the resurrection from the dead.

Philippians 3:7–11

The fellowship of sharing in his sufferings. That's a great mystery. Is there an empathy and depth of relationship with Christ that suffering alone brings? I think so. But sometimes, I admit, I'm afraid that when we view God with tearstained human eyes and a decimated heart, he just seems cruel.

IS GOD CRUEL?

I think of the woman who wrote to me about the death of her son. He had a heart attack at the age of forty-one. She sat by his bedside in the hospital, willing him to live. She called everyone she could think of who had any faith in God at all and asked them to pray. Her church had an all-night prayer vigil. She fasted and prayed for four days and four nights as she watched her boy fight for his life. He lost the fight.

"Why would God do that?" she wrote. "It would have been a small thing for him to touch my boy. He was a good boy. His wife needed him. His two children needed him. I loved him so much. He was my baby. Why? It says in the Bible, 'I tell you that if two of you on earth agree about anything you ask for, it will be done for you by my Father in heaven. For where two or three come together in my name, there am I with them' (Matthew 18:19–20). We did that, Sheila. There were more than two or three. We agreed on God healing my boy. Why would God put that in the Bible if it's not true? It says, 'It *will* be done.' Not, 'If it's God's will,' but '*It will be done.*' God did not keep his word. I have lost my anchor. I have lost hope. If I can't trust God, where am I?"

Her letter broke my heart. Her pain was so palpable it hit me like a blow to my solar plexus. I understood her words. They made total sense to me. I imagined bumping into her a few years down the line. This time it's her husband who is critically ill. What do I say to her? "Just trust God, Margaret! Put your husband in God's hands." Would she look at me as though I had suggested feeding a second baby to the dogs?

I turned again to a similar letter, written centuries before Margaret's and yet poured out from the same pen of pain:

> Hear my prayer, O LORD;
>> let my cry for help come to you.
> Do not hide your face from me
>> when I am in distress.
> Turn your ear to me;
>> when I call, answer me quickly.
>
> For my days vanish like smoke;
>> my bones burn like glowing embers.
> My heart is blighted and withered like grass;
>> I forget to eat my food.
> Because of my loud groaning
>> I am reduced to skin and bones.
> I am like a desert owl,
>> like an owl among the ruins.
> I lie awake; I have become
>> like a bird alone on a roof.
> All day long my enemies taunt me;
>> those who rail against me use my name as a curse.
> For I eat ashes as my food
>> and mingle my drink with tears
> because of your great wrath,
>> for you have taken me up and thrown me aside.
> My days are like the evening shadow;
>> I wither away like grass.
>
> *Psalm 102:1–11*

What a profound picture! *Forgetting to eat food. Reduced to skin and bones. A bird alone on a roof. Taunted and thrown aside. Withering away. A mere shadow.*

I saw this same kind of lonely terror in the face of a woman at the Anaheim conference in September of 1999.

"This weekend is the first anniversary of the death of my only child," she said. She whispered it in my ear. "He was killed in a car accident. His body was so badly destroyed that the only part they could show my husband and me to identify was his left hand."

A sob caught her voice and choked her into the silence of the owl among the ruins.

"I want your book for me and your music for my husband. He does not read anymore. He doesn't do much anymore. Perhaps your songs can reach into his pit."

I held her for a long time, consumed with the overwhelming question of how Barry and I would survive such an indecent assault if it had happened to us. At moments like this, I feel as though I stand with an empty breadbasket before those who are starving to death. She didn't ask "Why?" She didn't have to. The unanswerable question stood there as the unspoken lament of two mothers—a wail too deep for words.

For those who can voice it, the great "Why?" is perhaps the most difficult question I am ever asked as a Christian.

- If God can heal, why does he refuse to?
- If God is powerful, why is he so frugal with his power?
- If God says something in his Word, why can't I count on it?
- If God loves me, why doesn't he show it in ways I can see?

Silence in the face of these primal questions cause many to become so disillusioned with the person of God that whether he is real or not is no longer the issue. It's his character and ways they can no longer say yes to. Perhaps this seems blasphemous to you. We are taught in our Christian culture to say yes to God because it's the right thing to do. But when your life is left in ruins, old-time camp songs bring little comfort.

So, is God cruel? Why, we ask, would anyone who has the power to stop an evil allow it to progress?

One day Christian ran into the house calling for me to come into the yard. "It's a bird, Mommy! Help the bird!"

I ran into the backyard and saw that a terrified blue jay had one of its legs caught on the string of Christian's kite. It was struggling against the string wrapped around a fence post, and it couldn't free itself. Christian was crying. "Help the bird, Mommy!"

I approached the bird and, as gently as I could, took its leg in my hand and began to unwind the string. In terror the bird pecked at my hand, but finally it was free, and it took to the sky with wild abandon.

"Yeah, Mommy! We saved the bird," Christian cried.

Now every time we're in the yard, and we hear a bird cry out, Christian looks up and says, "You're welcome." He assumes his bird or one of its relatives has come back to say "Thanks!"

There is something about the picture of this bird caught in the kite string that has stayed with me. When I listen to stories of decimated lives or pore over tear-soaked mail, I picture this little bird struggling, helpless. Surely this is how we must seem to God. Poor little birds trying to free ourselves from the places we are held captive, pecking at God's hand in terror.

That's how the great writer Dietrich Bonhoeffer felt in his final days in prison before he was martyred for his faith. He poured out the fears of his soul in his diary:

> Restless and longing and sick,
> like a bird in a cage,
> struggling for breath, as though

hands were compressing my throat,
yearning for colors, for flowers,
for the voices of birds,
thirsting for words of kindness.

So why doesn't God just cut us free and let us fly? Is it supposed to be good for our souls to struggle? Tell that to the bird trapped in the kite string. Tell that to a man about to be put to death, isolated and afraid, cut off from all that is human, from all that he loves. It would be cruel, wouldn't it, to continue to let a creature suffer if you had the power to help?

Why doesn't God just cut us free and let us fly?

We don't talk about these things very much. It doesn't sound very "Christian." But these silent thoughts, fears, pain, and anger rumble around the cellars of our souls. The only way to clean out the cellar is to ask the questions, to shake our fists at what seems so cruel.

I think of Joni Eareckson Tada as a teenager with shattered dreams and a broken body. She was an athletic young woman, full of life, of hope, of carefree confidence in the future. One moment changed all this forever as she dove into the Chesapeake Bay and broke her neck. Joni and I talked recently about that first devastating year in the hospital.

"People wanted to give me answers," she said. "They would quote Romans 8:28, 'And we know that in all things God works for the good of those who love him, who have been called according to his purpose.' I heard that verse over and over, but it didn't help me one bit. It was as if they were rubbing salt in fresh, open wounds. Somehow I was supposed to be grateful and say yes to this destruction of all I had hoped for. You know, Sheila, answers are good for SATs or for Alex Trebek and the audio daily double, but they didn't comfort a scared teenager."

I looked into the eyes of this woman I love and value as a trusted friend. She has now spent more than thirty-three years in a wheelchair as a quadriplegic.

"I would panic in the middle of the night," she said. "I couldn't wipe my own nose or brush the tears out of my eyes. It would be dark in the room, and I would get claustrophobic. One night I cried out for the nurse to help me wipe my nose. It made the other patients who shared my room mad because I woke them up. I never did it again."

I asked her what she did instead when she felt this same panic about to strangle her.

"I sang. I sang 'Do not pass me by, Lord Jesus.' I wanted to be healed. I read the story in John's Gospel about the man who lay by the pool of Bethesda waiting for someone to put him in the water as the angel stirred the waters. 'You can do this, Lord,' I would cry out inside. 'I'm so young, please do this for me if you love me.' He did not. I waited night after night, month after month, and God did nothing. God did nothing."

We'll revisit Joni's life later on, but can you imagine the panic, the fear of spending the rest of your life trapped in a body that no longer works but with a mind still as alive as ever? There is a sculpture on the grounds of the Crystal Cathedral in Anaheim, California, that hits me like a sucker punch every time I see it. It's a statue of Job. He is writhing in pain, body twisted, face turned toward God. At the bottom the inscription reads, "But he knows the way that I take; when he has tested me, I will come forth as gold" (Job 23:10).

I think of Joni each time I look at this sculpture and inscription, and I wonder why the testing has to take so long and be so hard. When Joni lay as a frightened teen in the hospital, was God being cruel—or was he just too busy to notice?

IS GOD INDIFFERENT?

Perhaps that's it. God is not cruel. He is merely indifferent to human struggles in light of the "big picture."

I see my authentic self in children more than anywhere else. I watch a three-year-old boy being dragged through Chicago's O'Hare airport. He is yelling at the top of his lungs, tears dripping off his chin, but it's all a show because he knows he's going where his mom wants him to go, whether he yells and cries or not. After all, she's bigger than he is.

Is that how it is with God? Are we yelling and crying but going along anyway because God's the biggest and he's too busy to listen to every little story from Planet Earth?

I watch Christian as he tries to entertain a real kid lover (not!) on a flight. He mistakenly assumes that he can win this person over with his animal impressions. He starts slow, with a cow. *Moooooo*. No reaction. He moves on to a goat, a sheep, a tiger. Nothing. I tell him to be quiet and stop annoying the man. He looks at me as if I just don't get it. He's saved the big cahoona for the end. But, when his cross between Godzilla and some other prehistoric beast produces nothing more than the noisy shuffle of a newspaper, he is at a total loss. He has been as cute, as clever, as noisy as he knows how—and . . . nothing! He is momentarily speechless.

Is this how it is with God? We try to be as cute, as clever, and as noisy as we know how—and . . . nothing! God is not impressed. Our greatest efforts are totally ineffective, even bordering on annoying.

Is this what Job discovered? I have often quoted the end of his story as the great "answer" to his suffering. After forty-one chapters of Job's railing at God for allowing Satan to destroy everything he cared about, God pulls back the curtain for a moment and gives Job a glimpse at the "big picture." Job replies, "My ears had heard of you but now my eyes have seen you. Therefore I despise myself and repent in dust and ashes" (Job 42:5–6).

I've always used this as a great defense of suffering—the redemptiveness of suffering, the good news at the end of a tragic story, the "coming forth as gold" bit. Here you had a good man whose life was put in the shredder, and God allowed it. Then, in response to a glimpse at the behind-the-scenes power of the Almighty, Job makes this great declaration of faith. But sometimes I wonder. Was it really a great declaration of faith, or did Job just feel stupid and small? God doesn't answer any of Job's questions; he just does the big "Wizard of Oz" thing, flashing his awe-inspiring power. Was this a display of the great love and heart of God, or more of a "Who do you think you are, small fry!"? If this is how God is, no wonder we are reluctant to give him the human thumbs-up to anything he might allow to come our way.

So I lay out on the table of my soul all the pieces of the puzzle I've collected so far. It's an incomplete, confusing picture at first glance. I begin with the Word of God:

> Though I cry, "I've been wronged!" I get no response;
>   though I call for help, there is no justice.
>
> *Job 19:7*

Then I read:

> Are not five sparrows sold for two pennies? Yet not one of them is forgotten by God. Indeed, the very hairs of your head are all numbered. Don't be afraid; you are worth more than many sparrows.
>
> *Luke 12:6–7*

I go back to Job:

> But as a mountain erodes and crumbles
>   and as a rock is moved from its place,
> as water wears away stones

and torrents wash away the soil,
>   so you destroy man's hope.

Job 14:18–19

Turning ahead a few more pages I read:

A bruised reed he will not break,
>   and a smoldering wick he will not snuff out.
In faithfulness he will bring forth justice.

Isaiah 42:3

From the same heart of desperation, David writes:

I am worn out calling for help;
>   my throat is parched.
My eyes fail,
>   looking for my God.

Psalm 69:3

Then the psalmist makes this powerful declaration in Psalm 121:

I lift up my eyes to the hills—
>   where does my help come from?
My help comes from the LORD,
>   the Maker of heaven and earth.

He will not let your foot slip—
>   he who watches over you will not slumber;
indeed, he who watches over Israel
>   will neither slumber nor sleep.

The LORD watches over you—
>   the LORD is your shade at your right hand;
the sun will not harm you by day,
>   nor the moon by night.

The LORD will keep you from all harm—
>   he will watch over your life;
the LORD will watch over your coming and going
>   both now and forevermore.

God's people before us faced the same questions and battles we do. Cries of fear and of faith echo through the ages and resonate yet today.

A while back I talked to two women at the same Women of Faith conference. The first one told me her story: "My husband was killed ten weeks ago. He was hit by a car while he was on his bike. Why would God allow this to happen? What am I going to tell my two-year-old son and five-year-old daughter about God? Why should they love Someone who took away their daddy? Why should they love Someone who could have stopped it and didn't?"

A few minutes later I talked to a second woman who had experienced a similar devastating loss. "My son was hit by a drunk driver," she said. "He was in a coma for four days before he died. I gave my life to Christ in Intensive Care."

He was dying, but we were lost.

The pain-filled words of the first woman were still ringing in my ears. The second woman must have seen the shock in my eyes as she continued with her story.

"Yes! God did not call my boy home, but he received him home. He was the only one in the family who was a Christian. As we watched his life ebb away, a silent truth hung in the air like the morning star. My mute son was the only one who was not afraid of death. He knew where he was going. He had talked to us many times about the profound impact his relationship with Jesus Christ had on his life. He was dying, but we were lost.

"His father, three brothers, and I all gave our lives to Christ by his bedside. He never knew. He never regained consciousness. But we'll be together again one day soon."

I was left speechless by this song of faith in the midst of pain.

BOOK OF JOY

Open to me words of wisdom in the midst of life's dark days,
Take away my human blindness, give me eyes to see your ways.
I am weak without your goodness, I am lost without your light.
Word of God, sweet breath of heaven,
Shine upon this child tonight.

Open to me words of kindness when my heart is sad within,
Help me rise above the sorrow, singing songs of joy again.
I will lift my voice to worship, thankful for your gift of grace.
Word of peace, sweet breath of heaven,
Friend until I see your face.

Open now the halls of heaven to each child who seeks your face,
Mercy flowing like a river from the Christ who took our place.
Took our guilt and shame upon him, bore our pain upon the tree.
Word of life, sweet breath of heaven,
Love of every love to me.

Sheila Walsh

TELLING THE TRUTH

Barry, Christian, and I always travel together. We've done so ever since Christian was six weeks old. But in the fall of 1999, I took a three-day trip without them. We were at the end of our hectic year, and we were all tired and a bit under the weather. We had gotten back from a conference in Charlotte, North Carolina, on a Sunday night, and I was scheduled to leave for Dallas at 6:00 the next morning. Barry and I talked about whether I should break our custom and go by myself. I knew I'd be busy each day as we filmed the opening video for "Women of Faith 2000." It seemed to make more sense for everyone else to rest. My father-in-law, William, lives with us, so I felt comfortable that my boy would be fine with Daddy and Papa to take care of him.

While I was gone, I talked to Christian on the phone every morning and every evening, and sometimes at lunch as well. I had hidden three presents in different parts of the house, and each day I would tell him where to find a new one. He seemed to be doing well.

Then I got home. He was a little quiet. He told me what he had been doing, but I sensed, as mothers often do, that something was a bit off. That night as I was rocking him, I asked him if he was all right. He said he was just fine. I said to him, "You know, darling, sometimes you might be angry with Mommy or Daddy, and that's all right. You can tell us."

He looked at me for a moment and then gave me his little sign that he wanted to whisper something in my ear. I bent down.

"Mommy, I'm angry with you," he whispered. "You left me."

I hugged him and told him I was sorry. I rocked him and held him tight, thanking God that children are honest enough to let us into their pain so that moms and dads can share it. When Christian fell asleep that night, I thought about what he had done and how hard it would have been for me. I don't like to let people know they've hurt me. I don't like to make myself that vulnerable. I hate being *needy*, and yet I am. We all are.

One of the biggest challenges in my marriage is to let Barry into my disappointments. I expect him just to get it—which is, of course, unfair and unrealistic. Perhaps it's not so different with God. I'm learning to invite God into all my questions about him. I'm learning to crawl right up into the Father's lap and tell him that I'm angry, I'm afraid, I'm sad. We are invited to do that, you know. He will be there. He will hold us. Rather than diminishing our relationship with him, there will be a depth of intimacy born out of honesty, out of bringing our unseen self, our secret self, so full of questions and fears, to him.

We long to be superheroes for Christ, but inside we are frightened children. We are never completely what others see. We are never completely what we ourselves see. Dietrich Bonhoeffer captured this truth well. He lost his life at the hands of the Nazis during World War II in Europe. He wrote the masterly work *The Cost of Discipleship*. But in prison he wrote out his fears and laid them on a table. It seemed a poor spread to him, but the humanity of his words, his fears, and his self-doubt gives me courage. If he had written only words of triumph, he would have left me with the question "But how does someone who is afraid face death?" The fact that he bled a little on the pages for you and me is a gift. He wrote: "Am I really that of which other men tell of? Or am I only what I myself know of myself?" I would imagine that in eternity neither statement is true or relevant.

I remember as a young woman in London going to see a movie with someone I was dating. We were fairly fresh in our relationship, so our good sides were well polished. It was an okay movie; I actually thought it was a little dull and emotionally manipulative. When the lights went up, I realized that my date was sobbing into a handkerchief. The movie had connected with him on a level he had been trying to keep the lights out on.

Mike Yaconelli writes about this in an article called "The Secret Self." He says, "Somewhere in the side streets of the soul is a place where this secret self lives." This thought torments us. How many times have you thought, *If people really knew me!* The great irony is that we imagine we can keep the secret part of our soul disguised from God as well. What I love about Yaconelli's article is its conclusion. He imagines Dietrich Bonhoeffer walking from self-doubt and martyrdom all the way home: He "walks confidently into the open arms of his God who, it turns out, is a friend to Bonhoeffer's secret self . . . *as well as* to the self everyone admired."

This is radical and wonderful. God knows all that is true about us and is a friend to the face we show and the face we hide. He does not love us less for our human weaknesses.

So maybe it really is all right to tell the truth. To whisper our fears in God's ear. To wail, Why, why, why? Perhaps the only way to face our fears head-on and find his peace in the midst of them is to start putting them all out on the table. I wonder . . .

Part 2

FACING YOUR
FEARS

A FEARFUL PRAYER

Dear God,

Sometimes I wonder if I've gone too far. I relish my new-found freedom to tell the truth, but sometimes it seems nothing more than a new form of rebellion. Perhaps in my familiarity with your reputation for forgiveness I've stepped over a line in the sand that I didn't see. Where is the line between honesty and sinfulness? Is there a line? When do you wash your hands of us? Do you wash your hands of us? Are we ever just too much for you? Will there ever come a time when you turn out the lights of Home and leave us out here on our own?

Sheila

4

I Once Was Lost

Boldly I come before your throne,
To claim your mercy, immense and free.
No greater love will e'er be known;
For O, my God, it found out me!

Charles Wesley

Grace meets you where you are, but it doesn't leave you where it
found you.

Anne Lamott

The Lord is my shepherd, I shall not be in want.
    He makes me lie down in green pastures,
he leads me beside quiet waters,
    he restores my soul.

Psalm 23:1–3

Will you always welcome me home?

I was channel surfing one night, trying to figure out why it held such great appeal for my husband. Why would a man flick through ninety-seven channels when he has a *TV Guide* telling him what's on each channel? And why does he have to do it all over again whenever there's a commercial break? These are mysteries too deep for me.

Before I got to the twentieth channel I stopped surfing because I was getting dizzy. Somewhere along the way I had heard a comedian tell a story about his grandfather who had started to exercise at age seventy-five. "He walks two miles every day," he said. "He's just turned seventy-six, and we've no idea where he is. He must be miles away by now."

I laughed at the notion. Then I thought, *Why are you laughing? That's how you've lived much of your life.*

One of my greatest fears as a young Christian was that I'd lose my way, keep on walking in the wrong direction, and in the end miss God's will for my life. When I was a student at London Bible College, I had a friend named Steve, who believed it was God's will that I should marry him. I had no desire to marry him. For one thing, he wanted me to wear a scarf on my head, wear no makeup whatsoever, and have fifty-three children!

When I told him I was not worthy of his generous offer and that I would pass, he said I had missed God's will, and, what's more, nothing in my life would ever work out from that point on. For a while he had me worried—until I telephoned my mother, who told me not to believe such nonsense. But Steve's attempts to manipulate me fed into my belief that I was walking a narrow tightrope in my life. If I were to make one mistake, I would be lost forever. What if I got on the wrong bus and God's choice of a mate for me was on a different bus—would I be single all my life? What if God had decided to give me twenty-one years to come to the place of total surrender to him, and I didn't get there till twenty-two—was the whole game over? How patient will God be with me when I talk to him over and over about the same things, but I never bother to change? What if God gives each of us four hundred chances to get it right and that's it—at misstep #401 we've used up our portion of grace and there's no more?

I hear these kinds of questions all the time. It's the cry to know our purpose in life, combined with the fear that in a moment of ignorance or rebellion, we'll miss God's will and be miserable forever. Maybe we get only so many chances to come back home after we've wallowed with the pigs. I wonder if that's why we're afraid to talk too honestly with God, just in case he might say, "Off to hell with you, you reprobate!" Our fear is a bit ridiculous, though, when you think about it: He *is* God, after all, so there's a fairly good chance he knows what we're thinking anyway, wouldn't you say?!

If we are to find the courage to live an honest life before God, facing our fears and walking with *open* hands rather than hands that are grasping for control, we need to look at ourselves as we really are rather than as we wish we were. In *Our Many Selves* Elizabeth O'Connor observed, "We are only able to grow in our relationship with God to the extent that we are willing to know ourselves." And John Calvin wrote in his *Institutes of the Christian Religion*, "Our wisdom, insofar as it ought to be deemed true and solid wisdom, consists almost entirely of two parts: the knowledge of God and of ourselves."

> *In ways too painful to articulate, God has failed you, or you have failed him, and as far as you can see, the conversation is over.*

What I know is this: When I was supposedly at the best place in my life, I was totally miserable. I was on TV; I was a writer and a singer, doing all the things I love to do—but I was lost. I look back on that time in utter amazement at the grace of God that burst through my pathetic attempts to feel good about myself. He longed to show me his love, to teach me that life is not just about me being "happy." It's much bigger than that; it's much better than that. I spent so much energy trying to rid myself of the dull ache inside. I believed that if I could be "useful" to God and to others, then I would feel better about myself. Yet I never did.

As you read this book, perhaps you are bitter and disillusioned. You're not even sure why you're reading these words at all. In ways too painful to articulate, God has failed you, or you have failed him, and as far as you can see, the conversation is over. But maybe not.

I bought Christian a new puzzle recently. The pieces came in a wooden box with a picture of three bears in funny costumes on the cover. Inside there were about forty pieces to choose from, so you can make the bears look different each time you do the puzzle. You can choose different heads or jackets or shoes. We have a lot of fun making silly-looking bears.

One night I was tidying up Christian's toys after he had gone to sleep, and I came across the puzzle. He had pushed it under the sofa (his version of cleaning up). I smiled as I saw the way he'd left the bear—with a yellow jacket, a pink skirt, and a cowboy hat. I held it for a while and thought, *This is what we do to God.* We paste on him bits of our past. Our dad's temper. Our husband's disapproval. Our mother's criticism. A preacher's legalism. We add what we hear at church, what we remember from Sunday school, what someone told us about the wrath of God. All the good bits and the bad bits—the truth, the fantasy, and the lies we believe—make up our puzzle of God. Our distorted impressions make it almost impossible to throw open our arms unreservedly to him.

So what are we to do? Only *God* can help us change this picture. Perhaps if we could get to know a few people who have had a dynamic confrontation with the love of God, it would illuminate the face of God. So let's face our fears together as we look at the lives of some of our fellow travelers and see how they fared in their journeys. We will see ourselves in one or more of their stories, because whatever we fear and face today is not new. Throughout all of history we humans have struggled to trust God. From the moment our story began we have been trying to wrench control out of divine hands. But even when we go to the ends of the earth in an effort to run away from God, there is *always* a way home.

Let's take a fresh look at an old story of two lost sons and see what liberating truths we can mine.

THE SELFISH SON

There was a man who had two sons. The younger one said to his father, "Father, give me my share of the estate." So he divided his property between them.

Not long after that, the younger son got together all he had, set off for a distant country and there squandered his wealth in wild living. After he had spent everything, there was a severe famine in that whole country, and he began to be in need. So he went and hired himself out to a citizen of that country, who sent him to his fields to feed pigs. He longed to fill his stomach with the pods that the pigs were eating, but no one gave him anything.

When he came to his senses, he said, "How many of my father's hired men have food to spare, and here I am starving to death! I will set out and go back to my father and say to him: Father, I have sinned against heaven and against you. I am no longer worthy to be called your son; make me like one of your hired men." So he got up and went to his father.

Luke 15:11–20

I have been familiar with this story since I was a small child. Perhaps you have too. In Sunday school we called it the story of "The Prodigal Son," but I'm not sure this is entirely accurate. It's really the story of *two* lost boys who miss the whole point of what it means to be a son. If we place the story back into its historical context, we'll see a different picture— an incredible picture that's about as good as it gets down here.

Kenneth Bailey is an active lecturer on Middle Eastern New Testament studies and professor emeritus of New Testament at the Tantur Ecumenical Institute in Jerusalem. He is regarded as one of the finest experts in unlocking the cultural keys to Luke 15. In studying his writings I have discovered several things about these two sons that have deepened my understanding of the magnitude of God's love for his children and how willing he is to get his feet dirty in pursuit of our hearts—even when we have broken his.

"Father, give me my share of the estate." This was an outrageous request. In Middle Eastern culture it was equivalent to saying, "Father, I wish you were dead." Can you imagine for a moment how you would feel if your child came to you and made such a callous statement—*You gave me life, you fed and clothed me, nursed me through all my childhood illnesses, lost countless nights of sleep as you cared for me. Now I wish you were dead, so that I might have no obligation to you and just go on with my life.*

Think of the implications of this selfish son's request. His father was forced to sell half of what he owned in order to hand over cash to this child, who was about to walk off into the sunset, thinking nothing of the decimation at home and the humiliation his father would face in his community.

So the boy leaves, and he goes through the money—half of everything a wealthy father had built up over the years—in record time. What can he do now? Go home? Absolutely not. He knew that if he went home, the *qetsatsah* ceremony awaited him at the village gate. In those days if a Jewish son disgraced his father by taking his inheritance and losing it all to the Gentiles, he was no longer considered a son. If he ever tried to come home, he would be met at the entrance to his village by men carrying a large earthen jar filled with burned nuts and corn. The men would break it at his feet and, shouting his name aloud, declare that he was cut off from his people forever.

The prodigal son knew the consequences of disgracing his father. He knew them well—and yet he had still had the gall to leave his village with his father's inheritance in hand.

Isn't it amazing how reckless we can be with our lives at times? I feel it in my own soul. I don't trust myself as far as I could throw myself (and you need to know I'm not athletic!). It seems to me as though I live between heaven and hell on a daily basis. I see the way God uses my life to encourage his people, and yet I see this sinful, flawed, selfish woman in the mirror.

> Within my earthly temple there's a crowd:
> There's one of us that's humble, one that's proud,
> there's one that's brokenhearted for her sins,
> and one that unrepentant sits and grins.
> There's one that loves her neighbor as herself,
> And one that cares for naught but fame and self.
> From such perplexing care I would be free
> If I could once determine which is me.
>
> *Author unknown*

The trouble is, I'm *both* of these people. It's similar to what Fyodor Dostoyevski writes about in *The Brothers Karamazov*. Dmitri, one of the brothers, moans that Jezebel the harlot and the Virgin Mary both seem to reside within him, and his life would be so much simpler if he could just get rid of one of them. Don't we all feel this? Let's have an honest moment here: No matter how much we love God, no matter how good we look on the surface, our minds race in a million and one different directions. If our thought-lives were made available for all to see, most of us would be on the first flight to Mars. We're all the same; we just pretend we're not.

We're all the same; we just pretend we're not.

"All have turned away, they have together become worthless; there is no one who does good, not even one" (Romans 3:12). Not me. Not you.

Barbara Johnson often says we are only as sick as our secrets. This is so true. It's why I have a couple of women in my life who know the inside of my skin as well as my husband knows the outside. I don't yell from the rooftops what's true about my sinfulness, but I am blessed with good friends to confess to. I trust them enough to tell them the truth—not just about what I've done but also about what I fear I might do. I believe we are far less likely to live out our secret lives if they are brought before the throne of grace and shared with trusted sisters or brothers who won't judge us but who will pray regularly for us and love us fiercely.

My humanity, my vulnerability, my awareness of my "Achilles' heel" keep me on my knees, but I still lose sight of the bigger picture at times. Let me give you a recent example.

The evening before I was due to speak at a Women of Faith conference in Anaheim, California, I'd had a foolish but painful argument with a friend who was going to attend the conference. Both of us were hurt and angry—and I wasn't about to be the one to give in. The evening of the conference arrived, and I sat in the arena with a stone in my soul, surrounded by nineteen thousand women hungry to hear about the love of God.

I was heartsick. I looked out at the crowd and then at my own petty, selfish, controlling behavior, and I was overwhelmed by my own sinfulness. I left the stage just moments before I was due to speak and found Lana, our team's prayer intercessor, backstage.

"I can't do this!" I said. "How can I stand up in front of all these women and talk about the love and grace of God when my own behavior is so self-centered?!"

Lana said, "God woke me up this morning with a message for you, Sheila. I didn't understand it until now. God wants you to know he sees the no in your flesh but he hears the yes in your spirit."

This was a turning point for me. To receive the love and grace of God even before my friend and I were able to sit down and ask each other for forgiveness was a humbling and liberating moment. The graciousness of God to see beyond my wretched behavior to a soul that ached to love better was overwhelming. I deserved to have a jar of burned nuts and corn smashed at my feet and to hear God say, "You are no longer worthy to be part of this team. You are not even worthy to be my daughter!" I deserve this more often than I care to admit. It's what the prodigal son deserved; it's what he knew was facing him once he stepped foot onto the soil of his home village.

So the boy tried to find a job. The *only* way he could save face with his people was by returning with the money he had squandered. But he discovered the painful reality that friends are scarce when pockets are empty. No one gave him anything. His new job fed him—barely—and that was it. He had no savings; he had no hope of regaining the wealth he had lost. Quite simply, he was out of plans.

This is where the story becomes most interesting to me. I've always thought that in his misery this selfish boy repented of his bad behavior and humbly went home, but this doesn't seem to be the case. Think about the context in which Jesus tells this story. It's the final story in a trilogy. He tells the story of *the Lost Sheep*, *the Lost Coin*, and, finally, *the Lost Son*. In the first two stories the shepherd went after his sheep and the widow went after her coin. So what about the lost son? Did he really choose to come home with a repentant heart all by himself?

Kenneth Bailey points out that the boy's rehearsed speech sounds very contrived:

> "Father, I have sinned against heaven and against you. I am no longer worthy to be called your son; make me like one of your hired men."
>
> *Luke 15:18–19*

Sometimes we ask for forgiveness out of a true sense of remorse, heartsick at our sinful nature; at other times we pray out of a desire to escape from a sticky situation. Remember Pharaoh, who kept the children of Israel captive until God began to send plagues against him? Only when he was fed up with his punishment did he summon Moses and Aaron and say, "I have sinned against the LORD your God and against you" (Exodus 10:16).

When Jesus told these three parables, each one further underlined the point of the previous one. So if the prodigal son "came to his senses" all by himself, then Jesus contradicted what he taught in the first two stories. Bailey suggests that when Jesus used the analogy of a shepherd looking for a lost sheep, it has the effect of reminding us of Psalm 23:

> The LORD is my shepherd, I shall not be in want.
>> He makes me lie down in green pastures,
> he leads me beside quiet waters,
>> he restores my soul.
> He guides me in paths of righteousness
>> for his name's sake.

I studied Greek at seminary, but I avoided Hebrew the way you avoid a room full of people with the flu. Hebrew is such a complicated language. But I'm deeply indebted to those who have spent their lives studying this biblical language and can unpack for us the deepest meaning of some very important words. The Hebrew for "he restores my soul" is *nafshi yeshobeb*. It means, "he brings me back," or "he causes me to repent." This seems to be what Jesus is saying in this familiar story. *God* brings the boy back. The boy did not repent and return on his own. You see, the son had his speech prepared— and it was not a speech of genuine repentance but of manipulation. A number of Arabic translations of this phrase "When he came to his senses. . ." read, "He got smart." Not one of them says he was repentant.

We are so like children, thinking we can weasel our way out of our poor behavior with great emotional speeches. I remember as a child being caught taking money out of my mother's wallet. It wasn't much, perhaps the Scottish equivalent of fifty cents. I wanted to buy "peas in their pods" at the greengrocer and sit with the other kids and their bags of peas at The Black Six, our secret hangout.

We are so like children, thinking we can weasel our way out of our poor behavior with great emotional speeches.

That evening my mom noticed she was short on the change she knew she'd had in her purse. I panicked. (I would make a terrible bank robber!) I blurted out a pathetic confession and was sent to bed early. I lay for a while in misery, trying to figure out how I could fix this mess. Finally I went downstairs and said in my best "dying heroine" voice, "Mother, I know you don't like me anymore, but is it still in your heart to love me again someday?"

Pass out the Kleenex and the airline sick bags!

What I love about the story of a selfish boy who wastes everything that had been given to him and comes home with a "let's give this a shot" speech is that even knowing all this deceit was in his son's heart, the father welcomed him back.

> But while he was still a long way off, his father saw him and was filled with compassion for him; he ran to his son, threw his arms around him and kissed him. . . .
>
> The father said to his servants, "Quick! Bring the best robe and put it on him. Put a ring on his finger and sandals on his feet. Bring the fattened calf and kill it. Let's have a feast and celebrate. For this son of mine was dead and is alive again; he was lost and is found." So they began to celebrate.
>
> *Luke 15:20, 22–24*

God knows my recklessness and sees my unfaithfulness, and yet he stands with arms open wide to welcome me home. *God* is the one who calls me back. He whispers in my ear and then waits at the end of the road for me, eyes straining for a glimpse of me on the horizon. Even my best responses have nothing to do with *me*. They are a gift from a Father who has a heart huge enough to embrace the world.

> *Amazing grace! How sweet the sound—*
> *That saved a wretch like me!*
> *I once was lost but now am found,*
> *Was blind but now I see.*

More about our gracious Father later. For now, let's take a closer look at the other lost son.

THE SELF-RIGHTEOUS SON

> Meanwhile, the older son was in the field. When he came near the house, he heard music and dancing. So he called one of the servants and asked him what was going on. "Your brother has come," he replied, "and your father has killed the fattened calf because he has him back safe and sound."
>
> The older brother became angry and refused to go in. So his father went out and pleaded with him. But he answered his father, "Look! All these years I've been slaving for you and never disobeyed your orders. Yet you never gave me even a young goat so I could celebrate with my friends. But when this son of yours who has squandered your property with prostitutes comes home, you kill the fattened calf for him!"
>
> *Luke 15:25–30*

From childhood on I was taught in Sunday school that the elder brother was just a poor sport. His little brother made some bad choices, got into trouble, and came home in rags. If his own father could forgive the brother, why couldn't he?

But imagine, if you will, that you are this older child. Your father is obviously successful in his career, and he has provided everything the family could ever need. Then one day your younger brother breaks your dad's heart. He takes half of everything, doesn't look back, and leaves you with a decimated portion of property and a brokenhearted father. You are the one who sits across from Dad every day at breakfast and watches as he just picks at his food. You see him out in the fields, looking down the road, wondering if today might be the day. Will his boy come home today? You feel like screaming, "*I'm* still here, Dad! I never left. Am I not enough?"

I've read stories about the impact of a missing child on the lives of the children still at home. I've talked with kids whose brother or sister had died, killing a part of their parents with them. I can imagine them screaming, "It's not fair! It's just not fair! I did nothing wrong here. Why do I feel so lost and forgotten?"

Weeks turn to months. You come home one day, and you can hear something going on at the house. You ask a young boy who is out in the yard dancing with his buddies what's happening. Traditionally we have thought the elder son posed his question to a worker, a servant boy, but Kenneth Bailey writes that the Greek word *pais* can mean either "son," "servant," or "young lad." The word *son* would not apply. It would also seem that all the servants would be inside, assisting with the banquet. So the most likely translation here is that of *young lad*. To me this makes it even more humiliating. You have to ask a kid what's going on in your own home. It's not *just* the fact that the family "loser" is back that gets to you; it's that he's already back in his old place *as if nothing has changed*! And on top of that, he now lives off *your* half of the money. He's been forgiven, and he didn't have to do a single thing to earn his way back into his father's good graces. And to add even more to your torment, there's a party going on, and the calf they're eating should by rights be yours! You are so angry you can hardly breathe.

Your father comes out and invites you to come on in and join the party. You can't hold back another minute. "Look!" you say. "All these years I've been slaving for you and never disobeyed your orders. Yet you never gave me even a young goat so I could celebrate with my friends." You adamantly refuse to go in.

In those days, for a son to refuse to attend a banquet put on by his father was the equivalent of breaking relationship with him. But you've had about all you can take. The injustice of it eats at you like acid stripping the flesh off your very bones.

Can you relate to this young man's feelings? Can you be honest enough to voice them to God?

- How can you be so unfair?
- Why did you bless *her* with a child she didn't want, while I've prayed year after year and sit here with an empty womb and a hollow heart and a husband who looks at me every day thinking it's my fault?
- How can *she* have husband number two, and you've never even given me one!
- Would it really be so hard for you to give me a job that I love?
- Why did you heal that loser but let my wonderful husband who loved you die?
- Why do you bless other people but just pass right over me? I've spent my whole life trying to honor you, and you always seem to be throwing a party for someone else!
- You are not fair, God. You are just not fair!

What does the father say to this son who won't come in—this boy who is now so sick of it all he's prepared to be the one who humiliates his dad, because, after all, trying to honor Dad must just be a colossal waste of time?

"My son," the father said, "you are always with me, and everything I have is yours. But we had to celebrate and be glad, because this brother of yours was dead and is alive again; he was lost and is found."

Luke 15:31–32

My son! I love that. Our Father is so gracious that you and I can be selfish, egotistical, immoral, immature—and still God says to us, "Welcome home!" We can be self-righteous, angry, bitter, disappointed, and disillusioned—and still God says, "My son! My daughter!"

Perhaps you are like me, and you see yourself in *both* sons. I never outwardly rebelled. I didn't kick up my heels as a teenager and come dragging back home with scars and bruises. But there are many forms of rebellion. What I didn't act out in my physical body I often acted out in my mind. It's so easy to point the finger at the one whose sin is out there for all to see and to sit back in smug self-satisfaction nursing our cold hearts. But God knows our hearts—and our hearts are what he is after.

> *What I didn't act out in my physical body I often acted out in my mind.*

Until we see ourselves as we really are, we remain on the outskirts of the party. In fact, it's clear that we can be with the Father all our lives, but not be present at the party that celebrates redemption. How tragic! When I finally began to understand how black my heart is without Christ, I was overwhelmed. Drawing close to God in my humanness is a daily process for me. I have to choose over and over to turn around and come home. But always waiting for me is the Father who, in his great love and mercy, comes running to greet every lost child.

> *Amazing grace! How sweet the sound—*
> *That saved a wretch like me!*
> *I once was lost but now am found,*
> *Was blind but now I see.*

A LIGHT IN THE WINDOW

One of my most treasured possessions is a book by the Scottish writer Ian Maclaren titled *Beside the Bonnie Briar Bush*. Its first owner, according to the inside cover, was George Sewell Jr., who purchased it in 1898. It traveled on through various hands and then became a gift to me from Ruth Bell Graham in 1991. I treasure it because Ruth signed it for me, but I love it even more because it contains stories from my homeland.

I told the story of Lachlan Campbell and his daughter, Flora, in my devotional book, *Gifts for Your Soul*. But I want to take another look at it within the context of how the church still reacts to prodigals today. This story takes us back more than a hundred years to the Free Kirk (Church) of Drumtochty. It's called *The Transformation of Lachlan Campbell*.

In this small Scottish congregation the men ruled with an iron fist, adhering to every jot and tittle of the law. No man would even shave on the Sabbath, as this would be defined as "work." Lachlan in particular was a stern, judgmental man who was making life miserable for everyone around him, particularly his only daughter—and he was doing it all in the name of "living a God-fearing life."

If you've heard the story, you may remember that one night, at a meeting of the church council, Lachlan announced that he wished to bring a matter of discipline before the other men. He told them that a young woman had left home and had gone to live in London. He asked that her name be removed from the church roll. The name was Flora Campbell, his only daughter.

One of the council members, a man by the name of Burnbrae, refused to go along with this request. He said, "With the Lord there is mercy, and with Him there is plenteous redemption."

The young minister of the church took Lachlan to his study and asked him what had happened. Lachlan told him that Flora had left a note for her father, telling him how much she missed her dead mother and that she knew she was a disappointment to him because of her dancing and dressing and silly ways. She said she would never see him or her mother again in this world or the next. At this point in the letter the words had become smudged by her teardrops.

The minister informed Lachlan that this was not the letter of a bad girl, and he refused to take her name off the church roll.

"But I have blotted out her name from my Bible, where her mother's name is written and mine," Lachlan said as he left the study and went out into the cold, bleak night. No one could reach him. His graceless theology had left him frozen in despair and loneliness.

Meanwhile, one evening in London, Flora heard singing coming from the open doors of a church as she walked past. She felt compelled to go inside. The congregation was singing:

> *There is a fountain filled with blood*
> *Drawn from Immanuel's veins,*
> *And sinners plunged beneath that flood*
> *Lose all their guilty stains.*

The sermon that evening was focused on the story of the Prodigal Son. The preacher kept repeating one line over and over: "You are missed, you are missed, you are missed."

In her miserable loneliness, Flora decided to head for home. She had no idea what kind of reception she would receive. This is the great fear of every prodigal: *Will I be shunned? What if I'm rejected?* It's a painful thought to rumble round your heart, but it's far more painful to follow it through to its conclusion—to go home and have your worst fears realized. Flora knew her legalistic father well. But Flora took the step that every lost soul has to take if they would ever come home again. She got on the train to Scotland.

During that ten-hour trip, what went through her mind? How many times did she consider getting off and forgetting the whole thing? (I hear often of lost souls who cannot find the courage to take the risk of coming home and choose instead to take their own lives. I have tearstained letters from mothers and fathers whose lost children never made it home.) But Flora stayed on the train, and when it came into the station closest to home, she got off and began the long walk across the hills to her father's house.

As she climbed the final hill she saw a light on in the window. And Flora knew deep down that she was being welcomed home.

Unbeknownst to Flora, God had been at work in Drumtochty too. The same evening Flora was drawn into the London church, Lachlan had been confronted by a woman in his church who told him that *his* shame was far greater than his daughter's. "Woe is me if the Father had blotted out our names from the Book of Life when we wandered from his house!" she cried out.

God pierced the old man's heart, and in that moment he knew he was wrong. That night he set the lamp in his window to light the way should his daughter ever set out to come back home.

What Flora could not have known was that her heavenly Father had been talking with her earthly father, just as he had been with her. For God is in the business of honest conversations when we are ready for them.

There was a grand celebration that grace-filled night in Drumtochty—and in heaven.

Did you know that the only time we hear of heaven throwing a party is when a lost boy or girl, man or woman, comes home to the Father? *Her father fell on her neck and kissed her.*

God is willing to have honest, life-changing interactions with those who, in rebellion, wander away from home and mess up royally, as well as with those who self-righteously sit at home judging the rebellious. People just like Flora wandering the streets of London, like Lachlan sitting in self-righteous indignation in his cold Scottish cottage in the bleak hills, like you and me who long to get it right and yet get it wrong all the time.

He restores my soul. Praise be to the Lord, my shepherd.

Amazing grace! How sweet the sound—
That saved a wretch like me!
I once was lost but now am found,
Was blind but now I see.

Come on in to the Party!

The selfish brother and the self-righteous brother, Flora Campbell and her father Lachlan, other redeemed prodigals and bitter souls I've known and heard of, all give me reasons to believe that we *can* take the risk of facing our fear—of heading for home even when we dread what we think is waiting there for us. We can't guarantee the reception we'll get down here on earth, but we can be *absolutely* sure of the reception heaven offers.

If you've messed up and tried to come home, only to find yourself rejected, I ache for you. I ache to think of the millions of people who have fallen through the arms of the body of Christ, wounded and unable or unwilling to cry out for help for fear that they would be ostracized. But let me tell you this: There is a party going on in your honor, and it's being thrown by God Almighty. So get down on your knees and say, "Thank you." Buy yourself a party hat and a big cake, and invite some other lost souls to celebrate God's joy at your homecoming. Open your heart and open your ears, and you will hear, "My son! My daughter! Come on in to the party!"

FINALLY HOME

It's all so amazing, this love without measure
That pours from your heart every day.
When I, such a sinner, am plunged in your river of life
I am never the same.
And I'm laughing out loud,
For I'm finding out
Just who I am in you.
From the earth to the sky
You're my one treasure in life,
And I just can't believe what you've done.
I'm so thirsty for you
Till my heart overflows,
Till the gates of heaven are opened and I find myself
Finally home.

"Finally Home" written by Chris Eaton and John Hartley
© 2000 Dayspring Music, Inc. and SGO Music Publishing, Ltd.
All Rights Reserved. Used By Permission. International Rights Secured.

A Fearful Prayer

Lord,

It's cold out here. It's quiet. It's dark. Your Word says that you will not give us more temptation than we can bear. But, Lord, sometimes it's tempting to despair when life slams us against the concrete wall. Where are you? Not out there, over the edge into the darkness? Surely not! Tell me you're not out there. If you are, there is nowhere else for me to go but over the edge.

Your frightened daughter,
Sheila

5

POSTCARDS FROM
OVER THE EDGE

Hasten, O God, to save me;
O LORD, come quickly to help me....
But may all who seek you
rejoice and be glad in you;
may those who love your salvation always say,
"Let God be exalted!"
Yet I am poor and needy;
come quickly to me, O God.
You are my help and my deliverer;
O LORD, do not delay.

Psalm 70:1, 4–5

The risen life is not easy: it is also a dying life.

Thomas Merton

"Blessed is the man who does not fall away on account of me."
Jesus Christ—Luke 7:23

Will you give me more than I can bear?

November 22, 1999, 8:44 P.M.

I'm sitting at my computer spilling out my thoughts onto a screen because I don't know how else to fill the time until tomorrow morning.

The day begins innocently enough. I had been a little concerned about Christian. It had been five weeks since he'd had a bout with pneumonia. He was recovering fairly well, apart from the fact that he wasn't eating very well or sleeping through the night. He seems congested to me, and I had said to Barry after lunch, "I think I might call Dr. Ladd and just get his opinion on whether Christian should be doing better by now."

So I call and talk to the nurse. She tells us to bring him in. No big deal, just a precaution when something drags on for a while. Dr. Ladd sees us at 5:00 P.M. We talk about Christian's symptoms. The doctor listens to his chest; he checks his ears and throat. So far so good. As a parting thought I said, "He seems a little peaked to me. He's not usually so pale or tired-looking around his eyes."

"I think you're right," Dr. Ladd responds. "Let's have the nurse draw a little blood and do a quick check."

Christian isn't thrilled. All the way to the doctor's office, he had been asking, "I won't have to have a shot, will I, Mommy?" I had assured him he wouldn't need one.

The nurse takes a pinprick of blood from his finger, and he wails like any fine American male. "Is it over, Mommy? Is it over?"

"Yes, darling, it's over," I comfort him. I thought it was.

A few minutes later Dr. Ladd comes back in. He has a more somber look on his face than his usual casual, fun look reserved for his kid patients.

"Something's not good here," he begins. "I'm going to have to take three test tubes of blood and run some more tests."

Barry and I look at each other. I look at Christian. I had just told him it was all over—twice.

The nurse comes into the room to help. Dr. Ladd says to Barry, "I need you to hold his legs down tightly. Sheila, you need to hold his head completely still."

Christian begins to scream. "Mommy, hold me, hold me!" He is totally panicked. Unfortunately it takes some time for them to locate a vein that will oblige. Finally that part is over. I hold Christian as he sobs and sobs. I am amazed again that even though I had held him down, he is now clinging to me for comfort.

Dr. Ladd sits down. "We have to eliminate a few things here," he explains. "His blood count is way off."

"What things?" Barry asks. "We'd like to know."

"First we need to eliminate the big one. Cancer."

"Well, first we need to eliminate the big one," he replies. "Cancer."

I am numb. I can't think; I can't stop thinking. We sit and look at the doctor—we've been struck dumb.

"There's a list of about fifteen things this could be. We dread number one and we pray for number fifteen. I'll call you in the morning. We should know by then if it's 'one.'"

I put Christian's shirt back on. We pay our bill, and we get in the car.

"Mommy, I want to see Santa Claus!" Christian cries out. "You said if I was a good boy I could see Santa. Was I a good boy, Mommy?"

"The best boy, Boo," I reply, using his silly pet name.

We drive to the mall, where Santa's arrival seems to be getting earlier every year. We park and get out of the car. I feel like a robot. As we stand in line, Christian was patting a papier-mâché reindeer. I look at Barry for the first time since arriving at the mall.

"Are you all right?" I ask. It has been six months since we buried his mom. Cancer.

"I feel sick," he says.

"Me too," I reply.

We make it through the whole surreal "Santa thing" and drive home. Christian is listening to his "Veggie Tales" tape all the way home.

"God is bigger than the bogeyman," Larry the Cucumber sings. *Is he bigger than this?* I ask myself.

Barry and I whisper to each other. "Let's not say anything to your dad," I say, "until we know something."

"Of course not," he answers. We are quiet the rest of the way home. We make it through a Domino's Pizza dinner. (I can't think clearly enough to cook anything.) I have two plays going on in my head at the same time. One: Everything's fine. (We all still laugh at how well Christian made out in the midst of this false alarm. Got to sleep in Mommy and Daddy's bed that night. Got to eat candy, play football in the bathtub. You name it, it was possible that evening.) Two: Nothing is fine. Nothing will ever be fine again. How will we survive this? How many times will we have to hold our son down on a table? How do parents bear watching their child suffer over the long term? Stupid, irrational thoughts go through my head. *I'm going to quit writing and speaking. God is just giving me some new trial to talk about. I don't want it. If it means hurting my son, I don't want it. I'd rather scrub toilets at Kmart.*

So here I am now. Christian is tucked into our bed with his dad, wide-awake, watching one of his favorite videos, and I'm pouring my soul into a computer with no idea what tomorrow will bring for each of us.

It's 9:18 P.M. What will I do until tomorrow morning?

NIGHT TERRORS

November 23, 1999, 3:00 A.M.

It's so quiet where we live. That's why I love the countryside. I walk around the house. I pick up framed photos off the piano in the morning room: Barry, Christian, and me on an elephant at the zoo; all of us sitting on the beach in Florida with the waves washing over our feet. Life can change in an instant. I wonder how many other parents are awake tonight. Life provides memberships to too many strange clubs—and you have no memory of ever applying to them. Those who have lost children. Those who have cancer. Those who are blind. Those who have been abused. The terrifying list is endless.

I hear Christian call my name. I hurry back into the bedroom.

"Are you all right, sweetheart?" I ask.

"Sure, Mom. Hey, Mom, did you know that bugs don't wear hats?"

"I don't think I knew that," I reply.

"Check it out, Mom. It's wild!"

He goes to sleep. I go back to my office and turn on "The Lucy Show." I eat a pint of Häagen-Dazs vanilla ice cream without tasting any of it. I watch the sun rise. It looks like it's going to be a beautiful day. I can't wait for the phone to ring, and yet I dread it ringing. I try to prepare myself, but I don't know how. I feel like a terrified little girl. I go back into the bedroom to check on Christian. I want one last look at him before I'm told he might die. I look at Barry, curled up at an awkward angle. *He'll have a headache in the morning sleeping like that,* I think absently. The triviality of this thought makes me realize that we would give everything we have in the whole world if *that's* all we had to face in the morning.

I crawl back into bed, and Christian, like a heat-seeking missile, scoots over to my side and puts his head on my shoulder. Trust. Childlike innocence. *Please let him keep that, God. Please don't let needles and hospitals and grown-up words he can't understand steal that from him. I beg you, Father. I will take anything, anything you want to give me, if you'll just let him be okay. What will this do to William? Christian is his reason for living. He can't even bear to watch me take a splinter out of his foot. Why did you give us hearts when they are so susceptible to breaking? I can already hear the "comforting" words of others: "God has a plan in all of this"; "he will never give you more than you can bear"; "remember that all things work together for good."*

At 9:00 A.M. on the nose the phone rings. The world stops. Barry is in the kitchen. I hear him pick up the phone. I can hear my heartbeat in my head. He comes into the bedroom.

"No cancer!"

We don't say anything for a few seconds. The words hover in the air. I'm afraid to embrace them in case they vanish as I try to grasp them.

"What did they find?" I ask.

"Well, he's definitely anemic, and we have to take him back next Wednesday for a couple more tests—see if there's blood in his stool and a couple of other things."

"But 'the big one' is ruled out?"

"The big one is ruled out."

"Okay."

I don't know what to do with myself or my thoughts. I don't immediately feel the relief I would have expected. Do I thank God that my boy is okay? To do so almost implies that God decided to let us off the hook this time, but there's always tomorrow, when the next crisis awaits. What ticket will we get next time in the heavenly lottery? Chances of getting a winning ticket twice in a row are slim.

Yet I still bargain with God. Give it to me, not to him.

In the deepest part of my soul I don't believe that. I don't believe God is like that. I really believe he was up all night with me. I felt his presence as I looked at the photos, as I watched the sunrise—but it's so hard to embrace the painful moments of life when they wound those we love.

What did I see in myself during the long hard night? The most obvious—I am a mother who loves her son and can't bear the thought of him being in pain. I got a fresh sense of my feelings of helplessness and vulnerability, my own lack of control. But there was something else there this time that I don't remember from other long nights in the past. There was the sense of the companionship of God through the long hours till morning dawned. I felt free to pour out the entire contents of my soul. Yes! The whole contents of my soul *without* being afraid that my honesty would impact the news I received in the morning.

"Sorry, Sheila. You failed test #239 so your son gets cancer."

And yet I still bargain with God. *Give it to me, not to him.*

POSTCARD: OVER THE EDGE

I love Christmas letters because they help me get caught up with friends I don't get to see as often as I'd like. I keep them all in a box in my office. They are a cherished taste of the lives of those I love.

My friend Marilyn Lorenz writes a poem each year, updating her larger circle of friends on the year that has gone by in the lives of her family. I look forward to it every December. It's not Keats, but it's Marilyn. It has her unique stamp. I write our family's annual letter, but it's usually not from me. I have written it from the perspective of various pets through the years: the dog, the hamster, the Peruvian parrot, our cat, Lilly.

Not all letters make us smile, however. The letter that moved me most in December of 1999 was the one from the Schrauger family. My thoughts turned to them as I sat at my computer on my "longest night" and waited for the results of Christian's blood tests. I didn't want to think about them that night. I don't want to remember the look in Brian Schrauger's eyes when I bumped into him in a store the other evening— the pain lines etched on his face as he endures the torture of taking his son, Taylor, for another round of chemotherapy. Brian looked like a man who was drowning in the pool of his own pain.

In May of 1998, a liter-size osteosarcoma was discovered in ten-year-old Taylor's body. In August of that year the tumor was removed. In order to get it out in one piece, Taylor's left leg and pelvic bones were also removed. All scans were clear in February of 1999. A moment to breathe—just a moment. A moment to hope—just a moment.

June 1, 1999, the cancer is back. This time it's in Taylor's lung. More surgery. Five nodules were removed on August 2 and two nodules two weeks later. More chemotherapy.

September 21, 1999, a new nodule in his right lung and a five-centimeter mass in his lower pelvis. More chemo. The pelvic tumor grows as if mocking this darling boy who absorbs this deadly chemo-cocktail with the courage of five men.

Twenty-one more days of chemo were scheduled to take him right up to the night before Christmas Eve.

Where are you in all of this, Lord? How strong a grip do you have on Brian? What are you going to do about Taylor?

I never wanted to know how parents deal with cancer that tortures their child, pretending to be gone and then cruelly reappearing in even more devastating ways. I never *asked* to see this suffering close-up. It tears up my soul. But I can't escape one thing: The Schrauger family is acutely alive in the presence of death and all death's friends. All its many frightening friends.

Christmas Eve 1999 arrives. In our house, Christian is beside himself. He runs round and round the sofa, and every time he passes the fireplace he stops and looks up the chimney. "Nothing yet, Mom!" We put him to bed; he won't stay in bed. He is too excited. He has on his brand-new Night-before-Christmas pj's.

Finally, when I think he's fast asleep, Barry and William and I begin to assemble his toys and put batteries in the multitude of contraptions that are ravenous for batteries. William is working on *Rock & Roll Elmo*, a soft toy that plays the guitar and sings very loudly. He gets both batteries in place but makes the mistake of pressing the shiny black button. Suddenly, our quiet kitchen is turned into Madison Square Garden. The noise is deafening. William panics. He runs round and round the kitchen shaking the doll, trying to make it stop. I'm laughing so hard I can't walk. (As you know, women can't laugh and walk at the same time.) Finally he makes a dive for the guest bathroom, throws Elmo in, and closes the door. We finish up. It all looks so fun. We gather all of Christian's presents and put them on the kitchen table.

It reminds me of when I was a little girl, and Christmas morning was a breathtaking wonderland. We always did the same thing. Mum would go downstairs to report on whether Santa had come or not. My sister, Frances, my brother, Stephen, and I would stand at the top of the stairs in our pajamas, holding our breath until Mum made the great announcement. When she let us know he'd been to our house, we let out a corporate sigh of joyful relief. Obviously he had been kidding about that "naughty or nice" thing.

William and Barry go to bed, but I stay up for a few more moments to go over the menu for tomorrow. As I pass the refrigerator I see Taylor's photo, and once more I'm captivated by that infectious grin, spread across his face with such lavish abandon. I stop and think about him. I wonder how the latest round of chemotherapy went. I wonder how sick he is. I wonder how Brian and Debbie keep going. At Christmas 1998, they wrote in their letter,

> We've been to the edge of grief and fear. Completely helpless we've even gone over the edge, headfirst into darkness, the yawning void of despair. But we've never hit bottom. With lead in our souls and wingless, we've safely walked in storm-riddled air. Over the edge we've discovered a path—transparent but solid, unseen but real . . . very, very real.
>
> Like you, we too have often cried out, "Where's God?"
>
> His answer is clear—but hard to accept. "I'm here," he says. "Just over the edge."

Now it's been one more year of living out there, just over the edge. One more year of hope and disappointment—and the miracle of the fact that, although Taylor is so wounded in his body, his spirit is gloriously intact. A true miracle.

Brian wrote in the family's 1999 Christmas letter, "Faith is such a difficult thing; but in the end the discomfort of trusting God is weightless compared with the familiar burden of worry. Now if I could just remember that tomorrow ..." He signed off with a quote from Mother Teresa: "I know God will not give me anything I can't handle. I just wish he didn't trust me so much."

Brian Schrauger is a poignant writer. He has the gift of painting pictures with words that draw you into his world and put flesh on the raw skeleton of a family facing the unspeakable. I have been helped enormously by his honesty, his fear, his faith. He gave his friends this Christmas and New Year's prayer:

> *O God, Taylor belongs to you, not to us. Not even to himself. We know you love him even more than we do. Thank you for weeping with us, with him, in the face of this unspeakable horror.*
>
> *Because you've said so, we also acknowledge that in your all-powerful sovereignty you are a loving God who answers prayer. But you are God, not Aladdin.*
>
> *But this above all: In whatever way you deem best and with the help of your Spirit, glorify yourself in Taylor, in his brothers, in us. We are terrified by the implicit risk in this request. Help us, please. O Abba, help us. Broken, undone, we pray these things in Jesus' name. So be it.*

I am silent in the face of this stark, sacrificial prayer. There is nothing I can say. There is mystery at work here. God is here—but this is not the God of the easy life. This is not the God of parking spaces. This is not the God who performs tricks to entertain his children. *This is the God revealed by Christ.* This is the God to whom Christ prayed so intensely, blood running down his face like tears. This is the God Christ knew face-to-face, and so he prayed, "Father, if you are willing, take this cup from me; yet not my will, but yours be done" (Luke 22:42).

POSTCARD: FARTHER OVER THE EDGE

It's Tuesday. This means "Toddler Time" for Christian. Two days a week he goes to a play group at our church from 9:00 until 2:00. I resisted it until he was three. He is so fun to be with—but I know it's good for him to play with other boys and girls his age, as opposed to only his mother, who may be mentally his age at times but wears larger clothes.

I give him a big hug as I leave him with Miss Dawn, his teacher, and a bucket of Playdough. I have five free hours to write before I pick him up again. I drive to my favorite coffee spot, pull out my computer, and fire it up. While I'm waiting for the programs to load, I pull out a letter sent overnight the day before. It's from Debbie. I can't believe it. It's from Debbie!

If you've read my other books you have met Debbie. I met her almost ten years ago when I was the cohost of *The 700 Club*. I was drawn to her honesty and fascinated by anyone who would write to someone on Christian television and tell her she'd like to throw her shoe through the screen sometimes. I understood that dynamic. Television is a very flawed medium by which to communicate Christian truth. The very nature of a one-hour show leaves little room to portray the real struggles, fears, and failings of us all. Debbie was struggling simply to *survive*.

Initially, her diagnosis was multiple sclerosis, but it wasn't long before cancer ravaged her body as well. She flew in to visit me when I lived in Virginia Beach. I was horrified at first by her gaunt appearance. She weighed less than ninety pounds. But she possessed a wicked, lively sense of humor that illuminated her face like a two-hundred-watt lightbulb.

Each time I saw her she was weaker. I began to fly in to visit her at her home in Detroit. My most recent visit had been heartbreaking. She had lost most of her right leg to a strange, flesh-eating virus and was in extreme pain, despite the morphine pump in her shoulder. But she was still alive. By now she was tired of being alive. And to make matters worse, her father had just been diagnosed with a cancerous brain tumor.

This is too much, God! How much more can one soul bear?

I never knew what to say to Debbie. Her life, her pained existence, flew in the face of any of my sermonettes. But we laughed together and told each other bad jokes. I showed her my latest pictures of Christian, and she smiled.

"I can't do this much longer, Sheila," Debbie told me during our most recent visit. "I keep trying to be brave for my mom and dad, but I'm tired. I'm so tired."

I held her hand, and we sat for a while, in the presence of each other.

I held her hand, and we sat for a while, in the presence of each other.

"You will sing at my funeral, won't you?"

"Yes."

"And you'll sing 'It Is Well with My Soul'?"

"I'll try."

Christmas came and went with no card from Debbie. We hadn't talked in weeks. I felt terrible that I hadn't called. I wondered if she was still alive. I kept waiting for "just the right moment" to call, but there is no such thing. I was simply a coward. I was ashamed of being so negligent. I couldn't believe I had let my friend slip out of my life so easily.

And then, yesterday, my father-in-law told me there was a Federal Express letter on my desk. I ignored it, thinking it was routine business mail that could wait awhile. But this morning, with arms full of lunch box, coat, and Christian, I picked it up as I was leaving the house and discovered it was from Debbie.

Now I rip it open and pore over it. In typical Debbie fashion she comments on my Christmas letter from Lilly the cat, our family photo, all our news. Her letter is full of love and hugs for all. I read on. Her father has died. (I never thought he would go before her.) She writes, "Sheila, does it always hurt this much?" She is now receiving hospice care and knows her time is short. She reminds me of my promise about her memorial service and apologizes that her Christmas letter is late (!!!!!!). She was in so much pain in December that she *couldn't* write.

I think back to our very first meeting over a decade ago. She was in pain then. I couldn't hug her very tightly for fear that I would break one of her bones. But in the years since then I have seen her fly. I have watched her soul soar above hospital corridors and pain medication and up out of the reach of catheters and morphine pumps. She closes her letter with these thoughts, alluding to her father and my mother-in-law, who had died within days of each other:

> We are living between the already-has-been and the not-yet. The world looks at death and says, No more. We look at death and say, Not yet. Can we share stories with Eleanor and my dad? The world says, No more. We say, Not yet. Can we hug Eleanor and my dad? The world says, No more. We say, Not yet.
>
> You are always in my heart, my friend.
> Debbie

Through many dangers, toils, and snares,
I have already come;
'Tis grace hath brought me safe thus far,
And grace will lead me home.

POSTCARD: FROM WAY OVER THE EDGE

You are about to give birth to twins. When you first heard you were expecting two babies, you panicked—but that soon turned to outrageous joy and anticipation. At the first ultrasound you discover it's two boys. Your husband nearly self-combusts with pride. It's a perfect pregnancy. You get big—real big—but who cares. It's for the boys!

Finally, it's time. Labor is rough but not unbearable. Your husband is right there at your side, cheering you on like it's the Super Bowl and he's ready to catch the ball for the winning touchdown. You consider giving him an epidural injection in his head.

Then, there they are!! They are beautiful; they are perfect. You can't contain the joy. It spills over and splashes everyone in the room.

Then, something is wrong. Panic. Fear. What's happening? *Talk to me, tell me!*

These precious infants live for two hours, and then they are both gone, leaving a bottomless cavern in your soul.

I met this mom at a conference. I could hardly take her story in. I wept as she told me. She hugged me and thanked me for helping her. How on earth could anything I said have possibly helped her? I don't understand the mystery of how God works. I bring to Jesus my five loaves and two fish, and he feeds thousands as if they had been served filet mignon. It makes no sense to me. As I listen to this brokenhearted woman who somehow perseveres, I am struck again by the fact that I am on uncharted, holy ground. How does she endure? *How, Lord?* Perhaps she heard deep in her spirit Jesus' words to John the Baptist: "Blessed is the man who does not fall away on account of me" (Luke 7:23).

John the Baptist. Beloved cousin of Jesus the Christ. What fanfare ushered him into the world!

> "And you, my child, will be called a prophet of the Most High;
>   for you will go on before the Lord
>   to prepare the way for him,
> to give his people the knowledge of salvation
>   through the forgiveness of their sins,
> because of the tender mercy of our God,
>   by which the rising sun will come to us from heaven
> to shine on those living in darkness
>   and in the shadow of death,
> to guide our feet into the path of peace."
>
> And the child grew and became strong in spirit; and he lived in the desert until he appeared publicly to Israel.
>
> *Luke 1:76–80*

What cruelty took him out of the world! Look at the context in which Jesus uttered the words, "Blessed is the man who does not fall away on account of me." They were spoken about John the Baptist when he was about to be beheaded by Herod Antipas. Jesus called John the most remarkable man ever born to a woman (see Luke 7:28). John lived a very spartan life in the desert. He was a prophet with single vision. He knew his call: to prepare the way for the Lord. He was waiting for that historical moment when he would cry out, "Look, the Lamb of God, who takes away the sin of the world!" (John 1:29).

But in the end John was imprisoned. In those dark days in a miserable cell before his execution I wonder how Satan, the accuser, the father of lies, tormented him.

"You wasted your life, John. Jesus isn't the Messiah. You are a fool. You fasted too much. You've lost your mind. And now you're about to lose everything."

Just before he faced the executioner's sword, John asked his friends to do something for him. "Calling two of them, he sent them to the Lord to ask, 'Are you the one who was to come, or should we expect someone else?'" (Luke 7:19).

That's a strange question, isn't it? After all, John was the one who declared, "Look, the Lamb of God!" He saw the Holy Spirit descend on Jesus like a dove. Yet now he was asking, "Are you the one?" But the question isn't so strange when we consider that we enjoy the privilege of living after Jesus' resurrection. We know the whole outcome; John did not. He was dead before Jesus had even been arrested. I'm sure Jesus' forerunner had so many questions.

Jesus assured John's friends that he was, in fact, fulfilling the prophecy concerning the Messiah. "Go back and report to John what you have seen and heard: The blind receive sight, the lame walk, those who have leprosy are cured, the deaf hear, the dead are raised, and the good news is preached to the poor" (Luke 7:22). And then he adds these extraordinary words, "Blessed is the man who does not fall away on account of me."

In his marvelous book *The Prisoner in the Third Cell*, Gene Edwards talks about John the Baptist's last days and the adventure of living with a God we don't understand. Jesus healed many people—but not all. How would you have felt if you had waited in line for hours, and just as you got to Jesus, with your blind daughter by your side, he left? If he had just stayed one more minute, your girl could have been set free to live a normal life. But he left—and you had to take her back home, still blind. Now you watch her grow up and struggle; things that are easy for others are so difficult for her.

"Mom, you said this man would heal me! Why did you lie to me?"

> *Mystery. God's ways are far beyond me.*

Your husband, who has always been a bit of a skeptic, never steps foot in the synagogue again after this day. He drinks more. He talks less. Your sister has a birthday party for her daughter. You and your daughter attend. You watch the other kids run through the yard chasing each other; your girl sits under a tree. In your heart you're constantly worrying, *What will happen to her when I'm gone?* Every day for the rest of your life you remember the day God failed you. If only he had stayed for one more minute.

But his message comes to you: "Blessed are you if you do not fall away on account of me."

Put your own story in here. Trace the path of pain, the unanswered prayers, all the things that have hurt you, all the things you don't understand. Then think of John, who placed his head on the chopping block without ever having seen the risen Christ, and remember Jesus' words.

Mystery. God's ways are far beyond me. At times they seem far from loving. I've often thought that if I had the power to intervene in painful situations and change them, I would do so in a heartbeat. But I am a sinful, flawed woman who does not begin to comprehend our glorious God.

A strange thing happened to me recently in regard to this reality. I had begun to pray that God would give me his heart for people, so that I would see them with new eyes. I was staying at a hotel in downtown Cleveland during a Women of Faith event. On Friday morning I decided to go for a walk while Christian was taking a nap with his papa, William.

It was a lovely, sunny day. I bought a cup of coffee at a stand and was wandering back to the hotel when I realized that someone was talking to me. I stopped and turned around. It was a man about sixty years old. He was very dirty, wearing the badge of the homeless. I said, "I'm sorry, I didn't hear what you said. I was daydreaming."

"I just asked if you had any spare change," he replied.

"Oh, sure I do," I said, squatting down beside him to get my wallet out of my purse. I pulled out five dollars, gave it to him, and got up to leave.

Just then he grabbed my arm. "Do you realize what you gave me?" he asked. "Yes," I replied. "It was five dollars."

He took my hand and kissed it. "I thought you meant to give me a dollar."

As I walked away, tears began coursing down my face. I walked for a few more yards, and then I had to stop. I was almost doubled over with a weight of grief I have seldom felt. I wept for a long time. For the rest of the day all I could think was, *God, how do you bear it? How do you bear seeing all the pain of all the world, all at the same time?*

I believe God gave me a sand grain of insight into his huge heart that morning. Do I understand now why he works the way he does? By no means! But I know it breaks his heart when we hurt.

I am helped by John the Baptist. I am helped by the fact that he was the chosen one who saw the Spirit descend on Jesus Christ, and even John still had questions. I need the companionship of those who ask questions—which is why I love being part of the Women of Faith team. None of us is afraid to ask questions. It makes life so much less lonely. It's like living the story of *The Emperor's New Clothes*. Believers tend to invest so much effort in *pretending* we get it all, that we have a handle on God and suffering and all of life. Of course, this necessitates staying away from those who are suffering. What a huge relief it is to say instead, "Hello! The guy is naked! Doesn't anyone else see this?"

It's hard to be a spectator at the suffering of others. But I have watched so many broken-winged sparrows soar like eagles. Brian and Debbie Schrauger's honesty and vulnerability are almost painful to receive. To experience it pulls me back from mindless living to a desire to live and love intentionally. My dying friend Debbie is so alive that her very existence brings me to my knees.

These suffering people savor all their moments. They give weight to each day. Truthfully, part of me doesn't want to be that awake, that raw. Some days I think I prefer that God would be Aladdin. But that's not an option. This is the real world, and I do believe that God is good. So I stand on the edge of the edge and watch my broken-winged friends fly. It's a beautiful, breathtaking sight.

I am learning to say, "God, I love you! I don't get some of this stuff, but I love you. A lot of this isn't working, but I love you. With tears pouring down my face, with anguish and hope and even joy, I say Yes! I say Yes! to you."

"Go back and report to John,"

go back and report to Brian and Debbie,

go back and report to Debbie:

"Blessed is the man who does not fall away on account of me."

A FEARFUL PRAYER

Dear God,

Thank you for your unconditional love. I believe you love me and will always welcome me back into your gracious embrace. I know you will catch me when I fall over the edges of life. But what I still don't understand is, why let me fall at all? Why let anyone fall? What is the purpose of all the pain? Is there some redemptive element I'm missing here? Between the moment we enter this world screaming our lungs out and the moment of our final whisper, what is the point? I don't want to miss it, Lord, but I'm afraid.

Love,
Sheila

6

WRESTLING WITH GOD

How long, O LORD? Will you forget me forever?
How long will you hide your face from me?
How long must I wrestle with my thoughts
and every day have sorrow in my heart?
How long will my enemy triumph over me?

Psalm 13:1–2

Man has places in his heart which do not yet exist, and into them
enters suffering in order that they might have existence.

Leon Bloy

My eyes grow weak with sorrow;
they fail because of all my foes.
Away from me, all you who do evil,
for the LORD has heard my weeping.

Psalm 6:7–8

Is there a purpose in all of this?

I was very romantic as a teenager. Unfortunately, I was also overweight and had bad skin and greasy hair, so romance occurred only in my imagination.

I remember having a massive crush on the laboratory technician who worked in the chemistry lab at school. I think he was about twenty years old, and I was sixteen. I discovered through a few of the boys in my class who hung out with him that he was going to attend our annual school dance.

The movie began in my head at that very moment. It is the evening of the dance. I am standing in the corner of the room.

The moonlight is catching the golden highlights in my hair and yet at the same time disguising the rotundness of my waist and the breakout on my chin. I am talking to a few of the thin, popular girls when suddenly one says, "Look who's coming over!" They all turn to look while I keep staring at the moonlight. It's him! He smiles politely at the gorgeous girls and asks me if I would like to dance. The other girls part like the Red Sea to let me through. We dance on air. He gazes deeply into my eyes, confessing his profound affection for me. I smile, knowingly. The credits roll.

Well, part of it was accurate. I did stand in the corner of the room, for most of the evening, changing the records. He left after ten minutes with Belinda, who was seventeen and definitely not a Baptist, if you know what I mean.

My teenage years were filled with moments like this. I always liked boys who did not like me. I once went to a party at a friend's house because I knew Bobby Shields was going to be there, and I thought he was gorgeous. I bought a new silver blouse and black, slimming pants. Unfortunately he had been drinking before he arrived, as there was to be no alcohol at the party. When I saw him come in, I decided to be bold and go up and say hello. He attempted to reply and threw up all over my new blouse. He suddenly looked a lot less gorgeous.

One of the delicious ironies of my life is that when I hit forty and had my only child, my skin cleared up, and I ended up thinner than I was before I got pregnant. Finally! I was coming into my own. I was going to become one of those interesting, attractive older women. Then, because I have osteoporosis in my family, my doctor scheduled a bone density test. Bingo! Not only do I have osteoporosis in my spine, but I've already lost an inch in height. So, I'm going to end up thin, with good skin, but three feet tall!

As I've said, I was a romantic—but I was also very naive. The word *sex* never crossed my mind. When I imagined being swept away into the moonlight by the laboratory technician, I had no idea what we would do when we got there. This was not part of my dream. I remember when my poor mother tried to have the required "birds and bees" conversation with me. I stuck my fingers in my ears and ran out into the yard and hid behind the black currant bushes. I have spent a lot of my life with my fingers in my ears.

As a young woman I found my escape in books. I would read great tragic romances and imagine myself the ill-fated heroine. Angst was more familiar to me than easy victory. One of the books I most struggled with as a young, romantic Christian was a Graham Greene book, *The End of the Affair,* which was on our reading list for school. Greene taps into the human condition masterfully. The story had all the elements to pull me in. However, it disturbed me at the same time.

Sarah, the heroine, is married to a kind but boring man who never notices her. She falls in love with a passionate journalist, and they begin an affair. Sarah is torn between her love for Maurice and her guilt about breaking her covenantal promise to her husband, Henry.

The story takes place during World War II when London is being bombed nightly by Germany. During one of the worst nights Maurice's house is hit head-on, and Sarah watches in horror as her lover takes the full force of the blast and tumbles down the stairs, bloody and broken. She runs down after him, but it's clear to her that he is dead.

Sarah is not a religious woman, but in this desperate moment she asks God for a miracle to which she attaches a promise. She promises God that if he will spare Maurice's life, she will end the affair and never see him again.

Even as she is kneeling in prayer whispering her final pleading words, she hears Maurice's voice. He is standing behind her, alive. At that moment Sarah becomes convinced of the existence of God and walks away from the affair. She doesn't tell Maurice why she is walking away; she just doesn't look back. For two years she honors her promise but is tormented by it. Maurice is bitter and jealous.

As a young woman I had no sympathy for Sarah. As far as I could see, she was reaping the consequences of her own sinful choices. As for Maurice, I just thought he was the devil's tool. When I saw that a movie based on the book had been made in 1999 and was nominated for a Golden Globe award, I decided to reread it. I discovered that the passage of over twenty years had changed the way I viewed the central characters. I saw things I never saw before—the struggle, the agony, the pain of human sinfulness, the angst of being mortal. But there was another element I had missed before: I had missed the characters' wrestling with God.

As I pored over the pages, I saw that the central theme of the story is the compelling love of God that calls to us through the very cracks in our souls. Sarah is drawn in by it. Maurice fights it with every ounce of hatred he can muster, but finally even he has to acknowledge the presence of God. Unfortunately, it brings him no comfort. His will and God's will are diametrically opposed.

After two years of being separated from the woman he loves, Maurice hires a private detective to follow Sarah to see if there is anyone else in her life besides her husband. The detective reports that there is. What Maurice does not know is that Sarah is seeking spiritual help from a clergyman. The detective manages to gain entrance to Sarah's house and steals her diary, which he gives to Maurice. It details her spiritual journey, her promise to give up her lover, and the agony of this promise. Maurice is overjoyed. Another man would be hard to fight, but God? No problem! Maurice considers himself more than a match for this religious moment of weakness in Sarah's life.

He contacts her, and she, overwhelmed by her longing for love, goes to him. He has won. He is stronger than her fancy of a higher being who would hold her feet to the fire. Maurice is convinced there is no God. We make our own destiny; we choose our own happiness.

> *How can he pray for a miracle when he doesn't even believe that God exists?*

Within weeks, however, Sarah is diagnosed with a rampant cancer. In her weakened state she finds joy and peace in the presence of the love of God, the grace of God, the forgiveness of God. Not Maurice. He is enraged. He can't fight this. How can he pray for a miracle when he doesn't even believe that God exists?

Sarah dies. Maurice is alone, and yet he knows he is not alone. He ultimately acknowledges the presence of God as he has seen him in Sarah, but his final prayer is that God would leave him alone forever.

As I finished the book for the second time, I sat and wept for a while. My heart went out to each one of the characters. I ached for the husband, Henry, who was weak and knew it, but who really loved his wife and was broken by her death. I ached for Sarah and her humanity. The opportunity to sin is always there, and once you cross that line, you live forever with the scars of your decisions. You can find forgiveness and grace, even peace, but you are never the same again. You live with the broken pieces of your life and with the knowledge that the choices you have made ripple out into the lives of others. I ached for all the pain Sarah had brought upon herself.

But Maurice was the one I wept for. He was so talented, so handsome, and so out of control. I saw in him how offensive God is to those who don't want to believe. I saw in him how hard it is to come to faith when, if God does exist, he has taken away the one thing you most want in life. Why would you love someone like that? This is the fight, the wrestling with God.

Maurice's final prayer is that God would leave him alone forever. I found myself answering this prayer as I imagined God would:

> I can never leave you alone, my son. I love you too much. I ache with you. I hear your anger, but I see your pain, your fear. So I will keep on calling you as long as you have breath. I will call to you through the wind and the rain of your days, through your tears and your rage. Even as you shake your fist in my face I give you all I have. I give you myself. I give you ... my Son.

SLUGGING IT OUT WITH GOD

God's Word is full of honest struggle. The list of those who railed at God is extensive. Job called out to God from his bitter bed of pain.

> Why then did you bring me out of the womb?
>   I wish I had died before any eye saw me.
> If only I had never come into being,
>   or had been carried straight from the womb
>   to the grave!
> Are not my few days almost over?
>   Turn away from me so I can have a moment's joy
> before I go to the place of no return,
>   to the land of gloom and deep shadow,
> to the land of deepest night,

of deep shadow and disorder,
where even the light is like darkness.

Job 10:18–22

Such honest words did not sit well with those around Job. His four "friends" condemned his outbursts: "Your own mouth condemns you, not mine; your own lips testify against you" (Job 15:6).

It seems that little has changed. I received an e-mail message from Brian Schrauger today. It could have come from the text of Job. I had sent him a copy of chapter 5 of this book, in which I talk about his family. I wanted to make sure that what I wrote was accurate. His reply was humbling to me—and painful:

> Your chapter begins to reveal an un-talked-about side of God's mysterious and dark character (dark to me, dark to us): the part of him we cannot grasp and yet at the same time the part of him we are not summoned to approach with passive acceptance, passionless peace, superficial professions of joy and assurance. No, we are summoned to personal battle. This battle, this fight, isn't with the world, the flesh, or the devil, but is instead a messy, sweaty, bloody, painful, no-holds-barred wrestling match with God himself.

> This is the part of our relationship with God that we never sing about and almost never talk about—at least not in public, not from the pulpit. And yet these times of intense lament, even slugging it out with God, are encounters to which he himself summons me: messy, grunting, often loud wrestling matches to which he himself invites me to battle with nothing less than unfettered honesty, replete with malodorous sweat and bloody woundedness. Wrestling with all my feeble might—like Jacob, like Job, like Jesus.

Problem is, this divine summons, this gut-wrenching reality, makes most Christians (at least in the West) so intensely uncomfortable they either deny the summons, or when they see it in others judge it as heresy. Just think what would happen in most churches today if a person made it to the mike and said, "God has called me to do something I desperately don't want to do. In fact, the prospect of this mission evokes such anxiety I am often doubled over in physical pain. Sometimes capillaries even burst so that I sweat blood. I beg and beg and beg and beg for release. I'll do it if he insists, if he really wants me to do it. But, O God, please, please, please, let there be another way."

Such a person would be regarded, I think, as deeply flawed in his or her faith—a faith deemed insufficient at best, as clearly demonstrated by a sinful unwilling-ness, an unacceptance of God's perfect will, which in the end, after all, always works out for the good . . . right?

And if such a person in the very middle of fulfilling God's dreaded call cried out, "My God, my God, Why??? Why have you abandoned me?" Western evangelicalism would, with a patina of charity, nonethe-less in the end and in essence condemn him of heresy. Christ just wouldn't cut it with most Christians today.

Sheila, I write with the disturbing passion of a sweaty, smelly, angry, and very imperfect wrestler with God. You might think I am a man who has fallen away on account of Christ. But with the Spirit as my witness, I am not. I am, rather, a man who has fallen in with Christ, fallen into an intense, passionate struggle. A struggle to which Christ himself has summoned me. And a struggle, even while it continues, and in all my fallenness, in which he constantly assures me ... he is pleased.

Amazing.

God bless you. Much love to a fellow pilgrim who is no stranger to the dank, dark dungeon of the Giant—Despair.

Brian

I am humbled and proud to call such a wrestler my friend and brother. Brian has been told by some that his heartfelt cries to God are blasphemous, that they will make God turn away rather than lean in. But how will we ever break through the fear that consumes us if we cannot pour it out in its rawest form at the throne of grace? Where else will we go if we can't knock, knock, knock on heaven's door?

> *How will we ever break through the fear that consumes us if we cannot pour it out in its rawest form at the throne of grace?*

Simon Peter answered him, "Lord, to whom shall we go? You have the words of eternal life."

John 6:68

One of the things that was most disturbing to Eleanor, my mother-in-law, was the presence of children when she went in for her chemotherapy. It was a new world to her. Who could imagine that there are so many Little League wrestlers?

I asked her what was most troubling. "Their courage," she replied.

I see that, too, in Taylor Schrauger, through his father and the honesty that flows through his computer:

A couple of weeks ago, before going to Maryland, Taylor calls me at the office as he often does (three times so far today).

"Knock, Knock," he says.

With a groaning grin I consent, "Who's there?"

"Boo," he answers.

"Boo who?" I dutifully respond, mentally predicting the inevitable punch line.

But I am wrong. His concise retort is amazing, replete with wisdom beyond his years. Words from God through an eleven-year-old boy—a crippled, pain-racked kid armed only with the faith of WWJD bracelets and a lopsided grin; an underage bloodied knight, fully, valiantly engaged against a strong, old dragon—an ungodly beast which has already devoured a leg, a hip, and gleefully stabbed at young ribs, leaving huge, throbbing scars, beating painfully to the rhythm of a young boy's heart. Small victories have only ignited this ruthless creature's scaly maggot heart with a sadistic lust for nothing less than all the remains of Small Pilgrim's body . . .

"Don't cry," Taylor answers, "it's only life."

Stunned, I stutter with applause, telling him it is a line straight from God and for the record.

So off we go.

I run with a limp.

Taylor soars with a howl.

Together we cry and we knock.

Knock-knock.

Brian

Amen. Amen. Amen.

To wrestle with God does not mean that we have *lost* faith, but that we are *fighting* for it. Perhaps we have lost faith in our old familiar ways, familiar prayers, familiar assumptions about how life is supposed to work—but we have not lost faith in God. But who is this God? Who is this One who promises to keep our hearts and minds at peace? Who is this father who tells us he will be there when we fall?

Is It God, or the Easter Bunny?

It was October 10, 1999. It was supposed to be one of those special days in the lives of Christian parents. A holy moment. Barry and I are members of Christ Presbyterian Church in Nashville, Tennessee, and our pastor, Charles McGowan, was "bending the rules" a little for us to accommodate our ridiculous travel schedule. Once every three months our church holds a service of covenantal baptism. Parents offer their children to the Lord, asking for his blessing on their lives and committing themselves to raising them in a godly home. We have so many young families, so many babies, that there are usually between twenty and thirty children at each special service. We kept missing the designated quarterly Sunday. I was beginning to think Christian would be collecting social security by the time we were able to attend a scheduled baptismal service.

But then my mum was visiting from Scotland in October, so the church extended grace to us and said they would have a special service of baptism for Christian. I was excited that we would all be there together . . . Mommy, Daddy, Grandma, and Papa. We were to meet with our pastor in his study that morning at 8:30.

The big day arrived! I got up at 6:00 so I could get myself ready before getting Christian dressed. (A brief sidebar here if I may. This is one of the great unanswered questions of my universe: Why is it that if I have a day at home with nothing to do—a rare gift—Christian wakes up at 6:00 A.M. But when

I need to get him up at 7:00 A.M. for church, he is totally comatose, out cold? I suppose that question goes along with "Why do birds wait until you've finally had your car washed before they dump the contents of their last meal on your roof?" Deep, deep questions.)

Well, I finally roused my boy and got him into a bath.

"This is a very special day, darling."

"Why"? he asked as he was torpedoing his bathtub ducks with the tail of a large, ugly plastic crocodile.

"Well . . ." I began, trying to come up with a way to explain this to a two-and-a-half-year-old who does not like to get messed with. "Today Mommy and Daddy are going to ask God for his blessing on your life, and we will promise to take good care of you and teach you about Jesus and how much he loves you."

Christian was quiet for a moment, drinking it all in. Then he said, "I think I need a bigger crocodile."

My son is very opinionated about his clothes. He knows what he wants to wear and which ball cap goes with which pair of shoes. Barry is also opinionated about Christian's clothes. Unfortunately, their opinions often differ, as they did on this much-anticipated day. Barry had hired a photographer to be at the church. He had a clear picture in his mind about how everything was going to look. Ha! Ha! Ha! He had purchased a cream-colored silk outfit for this "moment in time." It consisted of a little shirt and knee-high pants with straps that go over the shoulders. Sort of like an anemic male version of Heidi.

I got Christian out of his bath and dried him off and started to put the outfit on.

"I'm not wearing that!" he said. "It's goofy . . . I'll look like a girl."

"Yes, you are wearing that!" Barry answered.

Let the games begin! I thought.

"No, I'm not! It's yucky, and I hate it! I'll wear my jammies."

High Noon continued for about ten more minutes. Finally I said to Barry, "Let me find something else that I know he'll wear. "

I reappeared with a new outfit that I knew Christian liked—a darling little shirt and pants with bears on them.

"Are you kidding!?" Barry exclaimed. "He can't be offered to God with bears on his pants!!"

"Do you have the actual Scripture reference for that?" I asked sarcastically. The day was turning into a full-blown disaster.

Finally we all agreed on a gray linen suit. By this point, Barry was steamed, I was mad at him (and on my third cup of Starbucks), Papa was hiding in his room praying for the return of Christ, and Grandma was sitting at the breakfast table with her head in a cup of tea. Christian had run back into the bathroom to get the crocodile so that he too could share in this special service. I had no idea if the crocodile was a Baptist or a Presbyterian.

We got into the car, running dangerously late by now. Barry put Christian into his car seat and said, "Listen to me! I want you to sit there, and I don't want to hear one word from you till we get to church."

Fat chance! You could have cut the atmosphere in the car with a knife. We sat in silence for about ten minutes. Then from the car seat I heard an unsolicited noise: "We represent the Lollipop Guild. . . ."

Christian went through the whole song from *The Wizard of Oz* at top volume. I sat there trying not to laugh till finally, by the grace of God, we all lost it. We laughed the rest of the way to church. *Perhaps this is going to be a good day after all*, I thought.

This thought, however, falls into the category of premature hope. Remember what Woody Allen says: "It's not the despair that gets you, it's the hope!"

Amazingly enough, we made it to the pastor's study on time and discovered that two adults and another little boy were being baptized as well. Pastor McGowan explained to us that the baptismal part would be at the beginning of the service. *Thank you, Jesus!* I silently prayed, grateful that we didn't have to sit through a long service with an unpredictable boy and a nondenominational crocodile.

After the first hymn, those who were being baptized were asked to come to the front of the church. The pastor explained that the two adults were being baptized as believers and the two children were being dedicated to the Lord by their parents. The adults were first.

As Charles laid his hands on the head of the first adult, Christian whispered—loudly—"What's he doing?"

I whispered in his ear—quietly—"He's praying for her."

He thought about that for a moment, and then, with a voice like a foghorn, he pointed at Charles and asked, "Is that God?" Muffled laughter rippled across the congregation.

Soon it was Boy Wonder's turn. I held Christian. Barry was at my side. My mom and William were just behind us, along with our good friends, Christian's godparents, Dan and Sara Posthuma. In Christian's defense I have to admit that Pastor McGowan scooped enough water in his hands for a fairly decent shampoo and deposited it on his head.

I saw it coming!

"Hey!" Christian squalled. "It's dripping down my neck. I already had a bath this morning. And you got it on my mommy's coat too!"

What a holy moment! Sara gave me a handkerchief to mop off our dripping son as we carted him to the toddler

Sunday school. As a parting shot he added, "He's definitely not God!"

Christian's declaration reminds me of a friend of mine whose daughter asked if they could have a heart-to-heart. "Of course, darling," she said, wondering what was coming next.

> *As a parting shot he added, "He's definitely not God!"*

"Mommy, I want to ask you something, and I want you to tell me the truth."

"Okay."

"Are you the Easter Bunny?"

"Well . . . yes, I am."

"Are you the Tooth Fairy?"

"Yes, darling."

"Are you Santa Claus?"

"Yes."

Her daughter paused for a moment, deep in thought, weighed down by this new information. Just as she was about to leave the room, she turned back and asked, *You're not God, are you?*

If God is not the man in the pulpit, the mommy that deposits gifts under the tree, the Wizard of Oz whom we hope will grant our every wish, then who is he and why should we trust him?

Painful Joys

The Women of Faith conference theme for 2000 was "Extravagant Grace." I wrote and rewrote my speech. I read it to my husband; I read it to the cat. Barry said it was too long; the cat sat in her litter box and said nothing.

Friday, January 29, arrived. I both anticipate and dread the first conference of each new year. Each participant has a new speech to deliver, and because I typically speak first on Friday nights, I'm the first lamb led to the slaughter. It's such an awesome privilege to speak to a half-million women a year. It's thrilling and terrifying at the same time. Each night before I get up to speak, I tell myself that this is *God's* thing. He is the one who puts it together, and unless he moves, we may as well all stay home and color our hair. I know this in my heart and spirit, but I still have to walk up those stairs and face thousands of women who have come, thirsty to hear from God.

I downed an illegal quantity of Imodium. The evening began. There was a glorious sense of God's presence in the arena. At the end of the evening I went to my book table. I signed books and talked to hundreds of people for a couple of hours. But the memory of one particular woman will stay with me forever.

That evening I'd told the story of our scare over Christian's blood test. I talked about my struggle with God through a long, lonely night—how I had walked the dark and quiet hallways and rooms of our home, dreading the call from the doctor the next morning. All 17,200 women sighed with me as I reported on the outcome of the doctor's phone call: Christian's cancer tests had come back negative.

I told the audience how I had wondered how many other parents were awake that evening. Then I met one.

This mom told me that this particular Friday was a year to the day on which she had paced the halls of her home, waiting for the results of her seven-year-old daughter's cancer test.

"*My* phone call was different, Sheila. The results came back positive. My little princess had cancer. I couldn't believe it. I was numb. I was afraid. I was angry. I was sick to the pit of my stomach."

I looked into her compassionate, compelling eyes as tears poured down my cheeks. We hugged for a few moments.

"There's something you need to know, Sheila. God's grace is there—whether the answer is the one we pray for or the one we dread. This has been the most difficult and yet the most joyful year of my life."

I guess she must have read the mystified look on my face. *How could a year like that be joyful?*

"I have seen Christ show up in my child's life in ways that are humbling and mysterious," she explained. "You don't expect to see such faith as I have witnessed in the life of a seven-year-old, but I have seen it with my own eyes. God is real. Grace is real. When you get back to your room, read Hebrews 11."

I thanked her for her precious gift to me and watched as she disappeared into the crowd, knowing that at the end of the weekend she would go home to a life that is not what she would have chosen and yet one that she cherishes. Such faith!

I went back to my hotel room that night and read these words:

> And what more shall I say? I do not have time to tell about Gideon, Barak, Samson, Jephthah, David, Samuel and the prophets, who through faith conquered kingdoms, administered justice, and gained what was promised; who shut the mouths of lions, quenched the fury of the flames, and escaped the edge of the sword; whose weakness was turned to strength; and who became powerful in battle and routed foreign armies. Women received back their dead, raised to life again. Others were tortured and refused to be released, so that they might gain a better resurrection. Some faced jeers and flogging, while still others were chained and put in prison. They were stoned; they were sawed in two; they were put to death by the sword. They went about in sheepskins and goatskins, destitute, persecuted and mistreated—the world was not worthy of them. They wandered in deserts and mountains, and in caves and holes in the ground.
>
> These were all commended for their faith, yet none of them received what had been promised. God had planned

something better for us so that only together with us would they be made perfect.

Hebrews 11:32–40

The world was not worthy of them. I see this in those around me who wrestle with God, bloodstained and broken, true worshipers. I went to Cincinnati to speak to over seventeen thousand women, and God sent *one* to speak to me—to speak to me in my insecurity and vulnerability, in my fear for my own child. I will never forget that woman or the look of love in her eyes that said to me, *This is not okay, but it is all right.*

Life is very lonely when we sit in our private dungeons of despair, whistling a song that, if we would only open up our lungs and let rip, we would hear it echoed from prison walls all around us.

In Christ we have the perfect pattern of One who told the truth, no matter the cost, who faced his fear, no matter the pain, and who found peace, perfect peace in the will of his Father. "Jesus called out with a loud voice, 'Father, into your hands I commit my spirit.' When he had said this, he breathed his last" (Luke 23:46). Jesus' words echoed the psalmist's. David was a man who had struggled and failed and struggled again. "Into your hands I commit my spirit; redeem me, O LORD, the God of truth" (Psalm 31:5).

Those seem to be the words of the finest wrestlers. Those seem to be the words of the greatest lovers of God.

Into your hands.

    Into your hands.

        Into your hands.

A PURPOSE?

As I look back over the course of 1999, I acknowledge that it was a year full of experiencing pain and walking with others who were in the midst of suffering. I admit I wasn't sorry to see it come to an end as I woke up on the morning of the last day of the century and flipped through a mental picture show of the past year. I remembered the agony of Eleanor's last few weeks in her battle with liver cancer. I recalled the disintegration of her body, her brave fight to survive, and the tender, intimate moments we shared. I thought of Brian and Debbie and Taylor. In my mind's eye I could see Taylor playing ball with his crutches, laughing and living loud. But with cancer the road ahead is always unclear. I remembered our scare with Christian. I wondered about my friend Debbie.

I knew that in an hour our friends Luci, Marilyn, Mary, and Ney would be arriving to welcome in a new millennium with us. I sat outside on the patio with a cup of coffee and my Bible. It was a lovely, fresh winter's day.

Quite a year, I think. *I really don't know what to think. So much loss. So many tears. I am changed by this year. I'm actually less afraid of death and illness and loss. I know I'll never be enough in my human shell to fully soothe the wounds of another. I'll never have all the right words to say, because for so much of life there simply are no words. I am more human this New Year's Eve than I was a year ago. I am more connected to others.*

I remember the verse from Hebrews 10 that had come to mean so much to me. I look it up in my Bible and read again:

> Let us hold unswervingly to the hope we profess, for he who promised is faithful. And let us consider how we may spur one another on toward love and good deeds. Let us not give up meeting together, as some are in the habit of doing, but let us encourage one another—and all the more as you see the Day approaching.
>
> *Hebrews 10:23–25*

In the last few days of his life Jesus gathered his friends together and told them this:

"My command is this: Love each other as I have loved you. Greater love has no one than this, that he lay down his life for his friends. You are my friends if you do what I command. I no longer call you servants, because a servant does not know his master's business. Instead, I have called you friends, for everything that I learned from my Father I have made known to you. You did not choose me, but I chose you and appointed you to go and bear fruit—fruit that will last. Then the Father will give you whatever you ask in my name. This is my command: Love each other."

John 15:12–17

Love each other as I have loved you.

This is a noble purpose. This is worth living for!

I find myself back at God's declaration in Jeremiah 29:11: "'For I know the plans I have for you,' declares the LORD, 'plans to prosper you and not to harm you, plans to give you hope and a future.'"

So what is hope? Hope is a very tangible thing. The meaning of hope isn't just some flimsy wishing. It's a firm confidence in God's promises—that he will ultimately set things right.

What is our future? Paul wrote that God has placed within our hearts a longing for what is not available down here, so that nothing else will do: "Now it is God who has made us for this very purpose and has given us the Spirit as a deposit, guaranteeing what is to come" (2 Corinthians 5:5). If you read this verse in Eugene Peterson's *The Message*, it says, "We've been given a glimpse of the real thing, our true home, our resurrection bodies! The Spirit of God whets our appetite by giving us a taste of what's ahead. He puts a little of heaven in our hearts so that we'll never settle for less."

This seems to be a key to defining our purpose. What we truly long for is just not available this side of heaven. For me this is strangely good news. It's like that annoying missing piece of a puzzle. As I continue to reinterpret the purpose of my life, gaining an understanding of this truth has been life-changing for me. I can stop spending every waking moment searching under the same cushions and through the same drawers for a piece that is not in my possession. I can give myself to something infinitely more worthwhile.

> *What we truly long for is just not available this side of heaven.*

With the steam rising from my cup of coffee, I gaze out to the horizon of a new century. *Perhaps part of the purpose of suffering is to teach us to reach out to each other,* I think. *To hold one another, to come out of our safe places and be a family.* Perhaps there are no answers at all down here, just each other. Perhaps *we* are the answer for now. We are the earthen vessels, the jars of clay, that bring the life and love of Christ to one another. We face our fears together.

Part 3

FINDING HIS PEACE

A FEARLESS PRAYER

Dearest God,

You are amazing! I love words, but I have none to fit you. I look at your face in the lives of those around me, and I am silenced by your "enoughness." I am humbled by your forgiveness. I am changed by your goodness.

I love you!
Sheila

7

THE FIERCE LOVE OF CHRIST

When you follow Christ, it must be a total burning of all your bridges behind you.

Billy Graham

Your righteousness reaches to the skies, O God,
  you who have done great things.
Who, O God, is like you?
Though you have made me see troubles, many and bitter,
  you will restore my life again;
from the depths of the earth
  you will again bring me up.

Psalm 71:19–20

God, who foresaw your tribulation, has specially armed you to go through it, not without pain but without stain.

C. S. Lewis

I'm finding power in surrender

It was late on a Friday night, and my feet were killing me. Four-inch heels get a little talkative by 10:00 P.M. I thought about taking them off, but then I sink from a fairly statuesque five feet seven inches to a "Stand up . . . Oh, you are standing up"—five feet three. I like to look people straight in the eye when I'm listening to them, and I have a better chance in heels. But it was the end of a long day.

After speaking that evening, I went to my book table to sign autographs and meet with anyone who wanted to talk. I'd been in line for an hour, and my dogs were barking, "Get these shoes off! Get these shoes off!" Then I saw her.

"Day by day, inch by inch. I'm not through it yet. I'm not sure I ever will be, but I'm here, and I'm glad to be alive."

At first I only saw half of her face, for she was turned to one side talking to a friend. She made it to the front of the line and turned her whole face around. I don't know if the shock registered in my eyes. If it did, she did not acknowledge it. She smiled and thanked me for my message. I looked in her eyes. They were bright and warm—but half of her face was missing.

"Can I ask you what happened to your face?"

"I was shot."

"What happened?"

"I was asleep one night and woke up to see a stranger standing at the end of my bed. I reached for the phone, and he shot me in the face. I don't remember much about the next couple of days. I was in and out of anesthesia. I've had thirty-two surgeries on my face, with more to come. I used to look a lot worse, if you can believe it!"

She laughed at her own dark joke. We hugged each other.

"How on earth do you make it through something like this?"

"Day by day, inch by inch. I'm not through it yet. I'm not sure I ever will be, but I'm here, and I'm glad to be alive."

We talked for a long time. Her story fascinated me. I could tell by the side of her face that was still intact that she had been an incredibly beautiful woman. Her appearance had been very important to her, she told me.

"I used to spend so much time on how I looked. I've canceled appointments with friends because I was having a bad hair day or a 'fat' day or a breakout on my chin. Then I no longer had a chin. That'll change a girl!"

I asked her how she managed to face a crowd of nineteen thousand women with such grace and confidence—and with such brutish scars.

"Christ's love." She said it with such simple beauty and integrity. "If you have spent your life measuring your worth by how you look, and you lose that, then you need to reevaluate everything. Down a long hard road I found that Christ loved the real me. He loves the part of my soul that is beautiful *and* the part that is scarred. I guess he will do the same with my face. I'm not ashamed anymore."

I wanted to climb the tallest building in Houston and kiss God's face! Who but God could do that? Who but God could take a woman obsessed with her looks and let her loss of them be the doorway to freedom?

"The other thing that was important for me was to forgive," she added.

"The man who shot you?"

"Him, yes. But not *just* him. Me, too. I could have beaten myself up for the rest of my life for living so frivolously for so long. I had to forgive myself also."

She showed me her whole face, and her soul as well! The whole face that had been the bomb site for another's madness or rage. The whole soul that had been to hell and back in the struggle to accept and forgive. She didn't favor her "good" side; she revealed it all.

I have been eternally impacted by this woman. How often do we hide from one another? How often do we show only part of our face and hide what we perceive to be flawed and ugly? What a gift of grace to be given so much from one who has lost so much!

I thought back to my days in college, and painful memories rippled over my heart. I have touched on the fact that I struggled with bad skin when I was growing up, but it was a huge deal to me at the time. I hated the way I looked. I knew that when people looked at me, that's all they saw. It was all *I* saw. I tried everything on the market to clear up my blemishes, but most of the products only made the condition worse. My internal view of my external self affected every aspect of how I lived my life. I favored darker corners in restaurants—no window tables, please. I turned down an offer of a camping trip because I didn't know how I would wash my face in the woods. I didn't want to wake up with others who would see me with no makeup on. My whole life became my face.

I've heard similar stories from others. From men who have lost their hair, to women who have lost their youthful beauty, to those whose extra pounds have eclipsed their lives. Living in America doesn't help. We are bombarded daily by media images of what beauty is according to the twenty-first century. But so much of it is smoke and mirrors. I know it is, because every time I have a photo shoot for a book cover or CD jacket, the art director will show me the photo they've chosen and ask me what I want to change. They can remove every wrinkle, add false nails, make my hair bigger or flippier. It's ridiculous. I don't get too carried away anymore. I reckon if too much is changed and then people meet me, they'll have a fit. When I'm too old to travel, I'll go back to major retouches and live in a fantasy world of my own, like Bette Davis in *Baby Jane*, and my son will pray for the return of Christ or move to China!

When I meet someone like the precious "flower" in Houston, my faith moves to a different level. It meets life head-on. The shallowness is squeezed out of my soul, and space is opened up for the Holy Spirit to live and breathe. Christ's presence is so tender in our "dying" rooms. In my small, colorless room in a psychiatric hospital, as my fears, my ego, and my carefully structured life lay dead around me, I heard the most beautiful love song of my life:

> Place me like a seal over your heart,
>   like a seal on your arm;
> for love is as strong as death,

its jealousy unyielding as the grave.
It burns like blazing fire,
    like a mighty flame.
Many waters cannot quench love;
    rivers cannot wash it away.
If one were to give
    all the wealth of his house for love,
    it would be utterly scorned.

                              Song of Songs 8:6–7

The love of Christ is a fierce thing. It can take the picture you have of yourself and burn it in the fire of his loving eyes, replacing it with a true masterpiece. When you begin to open to this embrace, you develop eyes for others. You start showing up in the lives of other people. You can be the first to offer love and grace, and not the one who stands needy and yearning on the sidelines. You can see yourself as merely mortal, even silly, but not be ashamed. You can have a makeup artist show up for your big, huge, important photo shoot with only blue Avon eye shadow in her makeup kit and see the whole woman, not just what's missing from her offerings.

A SNAPSHOT OF MY HEART

"Have you ever used this girl before?" I asked the agent in charge of the photo shoot.

"No. But I hear great things about her."

"From who?"

"Oh, people. People in the business."

"What business?"

"Our business."

It was my first book since I had gotten out of the hospital, so I wanted to look as "normal" as possible. My agent booked a photographer and makeup artist for the cover shot. I showed up at the appointed hour to discover that the artist had a smaller makeup kit than Mother Teresa—and only blue eye shadow inside it. Blue eye shadow! She asked me how I like to wear my hair, and I told her, "Kind of loose and soft." She got out her rollers. They were the small kind you use for a shampoo and set. The kind my mom uses. The kind Edith used on *All in the Family.*

Barry walked in just as she was beginning to tease my new "do." Torment it, actually. I caught him just before he combusted.

"Would you mind if I have a private moment with my husband?" I asked her.

"Take your time, little darlin'."

She left the room. Barry freaked.

"You look like a trucker's date! In a really bad part of town. This is a disaster. I need to talk to her."

"There's no point, Barry. She's giving us her best. She's sweet. Let's accept the fact that the shoot will be a bust and have a fun day. We will laugh about this later, trust me."

> *How kind of God to let me take a look at the heart surgery he is performing on me.*

It got worse. The photographer was part-time photographer, part-time clown. He kept waving fluffy things in my face to try to make me laugh. I could have maimed him.

The end results were hilarious. In the photos I look like I've just been arrested after getting drunk at a Tupperware convention. The great thing about the day for me, however, was that it contained a gift from God, a snapshot of my heart. If this whole episode had happened to me in earlier years, I would have totally panicked and made everyone, including myself, miserable. How kind of God to let me take a look at the heart surgery he is performing on me.

I love Brennan Manning's books. He writes with such heart, passion, and humanity. I read an article the other day in which he was quoted as saying that we spend so much of our time in the church trying to convince people to reach out with the love of Christ to others—to the least of the brothers. "But what if I should discover that the least of the brothers of Jesus," he writes, "the one crying out most desperately for reconciliation, forgiveness, and acceptance, is *me*? That I myself stand in need of the alms of my own kindness, that I myself am the enemy who must be loved, what then? Will I do for myself what I do for others?"

Forgiving ourselves is hard. But until we do I don't believe we can fully forgive anyone else. Forgiving ourselves means taking the step off the platform of self-reliance and out of ruby slippers and putting on worn, battered human shoes. It's accepting that we're *not* enough—and *never* will be—and being okay with that. Then we can accept others, knowing they are not enough either, and we can still have a gentle heart.

What do you think of when you imagine having a gentle heart? I used to think of it as being a bit weak, sugary-sweet, soft-spoken. But this isn't an accurate picture. In the New Testament, the most common Greek word for "gentle" is *prautes*. In *The Complete Word Study Dictionary: New Testament*, Spiros Zodhiates translates it as "an inward grace of the soul, a calmness toward God in particular. It is the acceptance of God's dealings with us, considering them as good in that they enhance the closeness of our relationship with him."

In *Living Beyond Yourself*, Beth Moore does a study on gentleness. She describes it as complete surrender to God's will and way in our life. "The term basically means to stop fighting God," she says. "It is quite the opposite of weakness. Meekness and gentleness is the power and strength created from submitting to God's will."

Isn't that beautiful?! My friend Betty Bradley describes this quality as "curiously strong." I love that. I want to be that kind of woman. I wonder if that's why God picked Mary to give birth to his Son. Was she "curiously strong"? She was only a teenager, probably around the age of thirteen. Imagine yourself as a teenager. Into your small world comes a magnificent messenger from God with some *very* radical news. You are to be the mother of the Son of God! You are engaged to be married. You live in a culture where if a girl were to become pregnant outside of marriage, her life was over. She was shunned by the whole community. She may as well become a prostitute. Gabriel spoke into this young girl's world, and this is what Mary said: "I am the Lord's servant. . . . May it be to me as you have said" (Luke 1:38).

Isn't that amazing?! Such faith and surrender! It's interesting, too, if you go back a few generations to a woman named Ruth. Ruth married into a Jewish family, but she was not a Jew. She was from Moab, which was a totally different culture, one that had no relationship with Yahweh, the Lord God Almighty. Then her husband died. Instead of going back to her culture and people, as Naomi, her mother-in-law, told her she should, she refused to leave Naomi. She embraced her mother-in-law's land, life, and God. She remarried a man named Boaz and had a child, Obed. Obed was Jesse's father, and Jesse was the father of the psalmist David. David, king of Israel for over forty years, was a direct ancestor of Jesus Christ (see Matthew 1). Ruth, a woman who lost so much as a young woman, took a leap of love and faith and became the king's grandmother, standing firmly in the lineage of the Messiah, Jesus.

BACK TO YES!

I look again at Dag Hammarskjöld's declaration of faith, and the light shines much brighter on it for me now. The "great cloud of witnesses" the writer of the book of Hebrews talks about (Hebrews 12:1) makes a very convincing case. The cloud of witnesses that surrounds my life causes me to sing for joy. The fingerprints of the work of God in my own heart and soul make me long for his touch more and more.

We used to sing "He is Lord, He is Lord" every week in our youth group; it was one of the only choruses with just three chords, and I can play just three chords on the guitar. Words. That's all they were to me back then. I thought I meant them; I just had no idea how weighty these words really are. It's like volunteering to walk Mrs. Beattie's imaginary pet, Tiny, and discovering that Tiny is an elephant. But the glorious thing is, once you get over your initial shock you begin to realize that Tiny wants to carry *you*. That's how Christ is.

You want it all?

Yes.

Everything?

Yes!

I'll have nothing left to hold on to. I'll have no power.

Here I am. Hold on to me. I have all power.

It was the fall of 1999. I sat in the radio studio, waiting for the morning show and my interview to begin. Someone on the production staff ran into the room and pushed some papers into my hand.

"Read this. I know you from your books. You'll love this!"

It was three pages photocopied from a Thornton Wilder play called *The Angel That Troubled the Waters*. I stuck the pages in my purse as we were about to begin the interview. I kept meaning to read them and never got to it, until recently. It is a powerful allegorical tale about a new invalid, a doctor who wants to be healed of his melancholy, who arrives at the pool of Bethesda and waits for the angel to stir the water. The angel reveals himself to the invalid but tells him to step back. The healing is not for him.

The newcomer begs for healing. The angel tells him again that this moment is not for him. Not now. The invalid tries to paint a picture for the angel of how powerful his service for God would be if only he were fully restored. The angel is silent for a moment. Then he says this: "Without your wound, where would your power be? ... The very angels themselves cannot persuade the wretched and blundering children on earth as can one human being broken on the wheels of living. In Love's service only the wounded soldiers can serve. Draw back."

Another soldier for Christ, William Stringfellow, offers an ethic for Christians—those who are aliens in a strange land: "In the face of death, live humanly. In the middle of chaos, celebrate the Word. Amidst babel, speak the truth. Confront the noise and verbiage and falsehood of death with the truth and potency and the efficacy of the Word of God. Know the Word, teach the Word, nurture the Word, preach the Word, defend the Word, incarnate the Word, do the Word, live the Word."

This reminds me of something my mother once told me. Every year my mum meets up with a bunch of her friends at the Keswick convention held in the beautiful English Lake District. One year one of the speakers was Dr. Graham Scroggie. He told a story about giving a message years earlier on the subject "Christ the Lord." As the hall cleared at the end of his message he noticed a young woman kneeling in prayer, obviously distressed. He went to speak with her.

"Oh, Dr. Scroggie, your message was so compelling, but I'm afraid that if I see Christ as Lord, it will mean changes I don't want to make."

He turned to a passage in the book of Acts where God told Peter to eat food that was unclean by Jewish standards. Peter said, "No, Lord." Dr. Scroggie said to the young woman, "It's possible to say 'no' and it's possible to say 'Lord,' but it's not possible to say 'No, Lord.'" He gave her his Bible, saying that he would go into another room and give her some time alone. He asked her to examine her heart and score out one word: either "no" or "Lord."

When he came back, she was praying; the tears were pouring down her face. The word "no" was scored out, and she was repeating over and over, "He is Lord. He is Lord!"

"I have told you these things, so that in me you may have peace. In this world you will have trouble. But take heart! I have overcome the world."

John 16:33

Amen. Amen. And Yes!

A FEARLESS PRAYER

Dear God,

Thank you! Thank you for putting such beautiful people in my life. The fragrance is overwhelming. The clouds are beginning to clear. The top of the mountain is still a long way off, but I can see it. I can see it!

Your daughter,
Sheila

8

THE OTHER SIDE
OF LETTING GO

The only thing we have to fear is fear itself.
Franklin Delano Roosevelt

He gives strength to the weary
*   and increases the power of the weak.*
Even youths grow tired and weary,
*   and young men stumble and fall;*
but those who hope in the LORD
*   will renew their strength.*
They will soar on wings like eagles;
*   they will run and not grow weary,*
*   they will walk and not be faint.*

Isaiah 40:29–31

How calmly may we commit ourselves to the hands of him who bears
up the world.

Jean Paul Richter

My vision is being transformed

I have not trusted magic shows since I was a child. My faith and gullibility were destroyed one day at the old fire station in my hometown. Every summer the station was transformed by a traveling troupe of actors who staged plays, shows, and talent competitions. I don't think my brother has ever forgiven me for making him duet with me on "I Could Have Danced All Night."

I was mesmerized by two ingredients of the production: the talent competition and the Good Fairy. She was in every play. I wanted to *be* the Good Fairy when I grew up. I would fly around the world with my magic wand doing good. I loved her with all my heart—until one dreadful Saturday morning.

> *With that kind of a vision we can fly forever . . . even with broken wings.*

The first half of the play was over, and I was onstage with all the other children who took part in the talent competition. As the emcee announced our names, we stepped forward and the audience applauded, according to how much they enjoyed each child's performance. When I stepped back after my bow, I stepped a little too far and landed behind the curtain where the fairy was sitting on a stool, legs wide apart smoking a cigarette. My Good Fairy days were over.

That's pretty well where I'm at as a Christian, too. My Good Fairy days are over. What I pray for now is the true vision of our Holy God that transforms our lives—the kind of revelation that was granted to Isaiah. Four words describe his "King Arthur, sword in the stone" moment: *I saw the Lord* (see Isaiah 6:1).

I can't imagine the sight, but I see the effect: "Then I heard the voice of the Lord saying, 'Whom shall I send? And who will go for us?' And I said, 'Here am I. Send me!'" (Isaiah 6:8).

With that kind of a vision we can fly forever . . . even with broken wings.

FLYING LESSONS

I would love to say that my first day on the ski slopes bordered on the pathetic. It did not. It dove right off the cliff into full-blown, absolute Patheticdom. I was in my thirties and went to Vail, Colorado, with three other people who were expert skiers. Why? I have no idea.

Day one. They headed for the black ski runs as I was still trying to get my skis on. I did, however, look just darling. My outfit was perfectly coordinated, right up to the little pink headband. I should have just stayed at the bottom of the mountain and leaned against a fence. But, no! I decided to try the slopes by myself . . . and without any ski instruction. I thought it was possible that I might be a natural athlete. How hard could it be to go downhill while perched on things that are slippery and pointing in that general direction anyway? I discovered that it really depends on if you want to go in any particular direction, and also if it's important to you to be able to stop when you approach a tree.

Day one was a disaster, so I signed up for ski instruction on day two. There were different levels. I signed up for Level One, "Total Moron." I was told to meet at the sign of the Bunny Rabbit at nine in the morning. Bunny rabbit! There were ten of us, and a sorry sight we were. All we had to do at first was get down a tiny slope. It really wasn't even a slope— just a gentle incline at the bottom of the mountain. I couldn't do it to save my life. Everyone else could. I was the most inept by a mile. At the end of the day my instructor, as he was knocking back the Advil, suggested I might want to get private instruction. (He added that he did not take individual clients.)

That night at dinner my friends regaled me with tales of racing down black diamond runs and sashaying around moguls (which apparently is not a breed of dog but a bump in a ski run). I said nothing. I just ate a lot.

Next morning I met the poor soul who was to be my teacher. We met at the "Baby Raccoon" area. My instructor was a cheerful sort. I knew I could change that.

He told me we were going to get on the ski lift. I was horrified.

"I can't ski!" I forcefully reminded him.

"We'll change that!"

"We'll see!"

The sight from the lift was breathtaking. Crisp, clean white snow lay all around me. *Please, Lord. Don't let me spoil this by spilling my nice, much-needed red corpuscles all over it!*

Getting off a chairlift is no easy task. As we approached the top I asked my perky teacher what I was supposed to do. He told me just to stand up and gently ski off. *But I can't ski, you comedian! That's why I'm paying you!*

It was humiliating to land in such an ungracious heap as three-year-old skiers whizzed past me. We sat at the top for a while and talked about the basics of what to do. He was a very sweet, patient man. We talked it over from every angle, then he said it was time for me to try.

"Perhaps tomorrow," I said. "I'll go back to the coffee shop and meditate about what you've taught me over a whole apple pie."

He was not amused. "Sheila, if you want to learn to ski, you're going to have to press through your fear and try. You'll fall, but you'll learn."

I still remember the terror I felt as I set off down that first beginner slope. I fell. I got up. I fell again. I got up. That's pretty well how it went all through the day, but I had a blast. By the end of the week I was skiing.

I'm skiing. Look at me! I ski. I am a skier!

I discovered that my instructor was a Christian. I think that's why he was put on Walsh detail. Only a man of faith could have taken me on. On the last day we skied down the mountain together, singing at the top of our lungs "In my heart there rings a melody." It was glorious.

One of the things I learned about skiing is that no matter how good you get at it, you still fall, you still get hurt, you have good days and bad days. But ask any skier, and they'll tell you it's the ride of your life. I am learning this about the rest of my life a little bit every day. Life is not the way I want it to be a lot of the time, but I do believe that pushing through my fear and heading down the mountain is the only way to live. I wanted it to be easier than this. It's not. Saying yes to God is much more difficult than I thought it would be. But it's also exhilarating.

I didn't go back to the slopes for three years. I assumed I would pick up where I had left off. Wrong. I was almost back at square one. I couldn't believe how afraid I was again. I learned another important lesson on the first day back: Don't take a break halfway down a hill. You do so at your own peril.

On one of my first runs down the mountain I panicked and made myself fall over (yeah, right!) so that I would stop. Then, like an idiot, I stood up, dusted myself off, and just stood there. I couldn't go up—and I certainly wasn't going down. I decided I would stand there until Christ returned and he could just pick me up on his way home. Expert skiers zipped around me, giving me a dizzying array of dirty looks, which I returned with the confident smile of the soon-to-be-raptured. Unfortunately, there was another inept skier coming down behind me who moved me to a new category: the soon-to-be-ruptured. I heard her yelling and waving her poles. "I can't go around you! Move! Move!"

I couldn't move. I just stood there like a deer frozen in the headlights. She slammed into me, and I hit a fence and broke my right thumb. It has never healed properly. Every time I get my nails done, if the nail technician twists my thumb around to get a better angle to file from, I get a twinge of pain. It's an interesting reminder to me of our calling in life. We have to keep moving. We have to keep pressing on. We have to keep doing what we know we can't do *apart from Christ*. Even then we will get hurt and carry reminders in our body and soul of the pain of life. But I am, as you know by this point, a fan of the wounded who carry their scars bravely and who follow Christ with an ever-increasing passion.

Our gossamer-thin lives are held together by the glue of God's grace.

I find myself in a very privileged position. I get to hear the stories of thousands of people who have taken that step off the mountain. Every week God speaks very personally to me through one of his "living letters," sometimes in a floral dress, sometimes in a leather jacket, and I am reminded of what it looks like to keep on flying—even when my wings are singed. It's clear to me that our gossamer-thin lives are held together by the glue of God's grace.

This is part of a conversation overheard on a bus:

"What are you reading?"
"A book a friend gave me. Said it changed her life."
"What's it about?"
The woman looked at the chapter titles. "Discipline," "Love," "Grace."
"What's 'Grace'?"
"I don't know. I haven't got to that yet."

But it's time. It's time to get to grace, to joy, to peace. Once we have found the courage to tell the whole truth, to face our fears, we are ready. It's what we are longing for and what we have been promised: "For the kingdom of God is not a matter of eating and drinking, but of righteousness, peace and joy in the Holy Spirit" (Romans 14:17). This is to be the hallmark of our lives as God's children. It's not something we can work up by ourselves or find in the *Five Minutes to Peace* handbook. Peace is a fruit of the Spirit. It has to grow.

The amazing thing is that it grows in such an unfriendly climate. You stick a mother in an intensive care unit watching over her child—and the last thing you'd expect is peace. But there it is all over her, mixed in with the tears and the sadness. You take a man's job away from him, the source of a significant portion of his identity, his ability to take care of his family—and peace would seem out of place, even unwelcome. But there it is. I have seen it so many times. The record stands for itself. It is a gift.

> "Peace I leave with you; my peace I give you. I do not give to you as the world gives. Do not let your hearts be troubled and do not be afraid."
>
> *John 14:27*

CAN I HAVE A WITNESS?

Let's revisit some of our friends from earlier chapters.

JONI. We left Joni Eareckson Tada as a frightened girl, paralyzed, terrified, lying helpless in a hospital bed. She sang softly to the Lord throughout the long dark night. *Do not pass me by, Lord Jesus. Do not pass me by.* She wanted to be healed. She begged God to heal her. She bargained and wrestled. God did not heal her. Later she would read the story of the man who lay by the pool of Bethesda (see John 5:1–9), and she'd ask God again to stir the waters. *Send an angel, Lord. Take me out of this bed.* But he did not.

Thirty years later she and her husband, Ken, were on a trip to Israel on behalf of her ministry, Wheels for the World. They took a quiet moment off alone, away from the crowd.

"Ken, look!" Joni exclaimed. "Do you know what this is? Do you see where we are?"

Ken drew closer.

"It's the ruins of the pool of Bethesda," she said. "Here I am, after all these years in a wheelchair. I am here in the very spot."

What a moment! I can't imagine what it must have felt like. Did it comfort or torment her?

She told me this story in the summer of 1999, ending with these words: "You know, Sheila. I've been in this wheelchair for over thirty years. Thirty years of being unable to brush my teeth or blow my nose or touch my husband's face. But God has used this chair to teach me how to love Christ. I am a different woman because of this chair."

There is a luminous quality about Joni's life that is hard to ignore. I ache for the pain of the heavy cross she has carried for so long, but I see in her soul a shining diamond that makes God sing for joy. Joni is one of the most joyful people I know. Whenever we talk, we end up singing. It's her life.

What a witness.

ELEANOR. I saw peace come to stay with my mother-in-law at the most unexpected moment. She grew up afraid of illness, of cancer, of loss. But in that very theater—that *cinema noir* where darkness and desperation reign—peace came. I will always remember her last few words: *I'm ready now. I'm ready. I'm not afraid.*

What a witness.

JOB. An oft-quoted source on the subject of suffering. Surely the poster child for human affliction. But listen to Job speak one sentence that is deeper than an ocean: "My ears had heard of you but now my eyes have seen you" (Job 42:5). The difference between what you know to be true and what you *know* to be true because you have been changed by it.

"After this, Job lived a hundred and forty years; he saw his children and their children to the fourth generation. And so he died, old and full of years" (Job 42:16).

What a witness.

BRIAN AND TAYLOR. One Thanksgiving day, Brian and his family visited his brother. Like many backyards nowadays, this one contained a trampoline. Brian writes:

> Taylor bursts out onto the deck on Thanksgiving afternoon. "My turn!" he gleefully shouts.
>
> Taking off a well-worn shoe, he hops over, hops up, and, on his solitary leg, bounces higher, higher and . . . higher—with perfect balance and enthusiastic delight.
>
> "Come on, Dad, jump with me!" he insists.
>
> We haven't done this for more than two years. And so I join him.
>
> Trampolines, like life, are full of risks. Rules help minimize the risks but, as I'm learning, never eliminate them.
>
> Pay attention, heart: There is no life without risk. And without risk, there is no life, no real living.
>
> My fun-loving, wounded son is not delusional. He is, in fact, amazingly aware and refreshingly sane.
>
> And so even in despair I am compelled to admit this thing called *Love* is real. And because it's real, death isn't all there is. It can't be. Death is not the last tomorrow.

What a witness.

KING DAVID. I take a break from writing to meet my friend, Steve Lorenz, for lunch. Sometimes we do small talk.

Not today. I have some serious things on my mind. He has been a source of wisdom and joy in my life since my emotional crash and my rebirth, so I value his perspective and his knowledge of the jigsaw pieces of my life.

I am supposed to be going on a trip to Ghana with World Vision on behalf of Women of Faith. Barry does not want me to go. I am excited about the trip and see it as part of my calling; he is aware of the potential hazards and how much my son would miss his mommy if she were gone for a week. So last night Barry and I got into an ugly argument.

"I don't think you should go," Barry pronounced.

"Why are you telling me this now, only three weeks before the trip?"

"I told you all along you shouldn't go."

"No, you didn't."

"You'll get sick, and your schedule is busy enough already."

"Why are you telling me now and not a month ago?"

"Think about Christian."

It got uglier then. We gave up, and, ignoring the scriptural admonition, we went to bed. I nursed my wrath. By morning I was miserable. I canceled the trip.

Over lunch Steve and I talk about control and relinquishment. Every time I think I'm really flying now, really getting this "Christian life" thing down pat, I hit another mountain of my own sinfulness and lack of surrender. I believe that the ultimate purpose of my life is to become like Christ—but to become like Christ seems impossible at times. I have too much baggage. I am too sinful, too stubborn, too controlling. Then there are moments when I get a fresh glimpse of the greatness of God, and I have a renewed sense of commitment and perseverance. I dance between those two realities every day. In *all* the moments of my life I long to live with eyes washed with a vision of Christ, but I lie down with "me" in the evening and I get up with "me" in the morning—and "me" is the problem.

But the call to become like Christ comes from a God who knows what each day holds for us. Remember?

> O Lord, you have searched me
> and you know me.
> You know when I sit and when I rise;
> you perceive my thoughts from afar.
> You discern my going out and my lying down;
> you are familiar with all my ways.
> Before a word is on my tongue
> you know it completely, O Lord.
> You hem me in—behind and before;
> you have laid your hand upon me.
>
> *Psalm 139:1–5*

Steve and I talk about submission to God and grace with one another. We don't dwell on the specifics of the argument Barry and I had. It's almost irrelevant. What I want to look at is the condition of my own heart. What I hate about these kinds of arguments is that no matter who is right or wrong, my sinful nature is exposed. I fall so far short of taking the high road; I sink back to the bottom of the barrel with amazing ease.

What I want to look at is the condition of my own heart.

Steve reminds me of the book *A Tale of Three Kings* by Gene Edwards, a little volume that has influenced both of us. The whole thrust of the message is *trust* and *control*. It's the story of Saul and David. Gene contrasts their different styles of leadership. Saul grabs hold of power; David holds it lightly. David is utterly convinced that God is in control, and so he lives with fear but is not ruled by it. His heart's conviction is that if God is through with him as king, then he is truly finished, but if God still has a purpose for his life, then all the armies in the world can't stop it from being accomplished.

Writer Anne Lamott told me about the saying in Alcoholics Anonymous that there is *your* will and *God's* will—and your will doesn't matter! Steve and I talk about the outrageous freedom this reality brings. Can you imagine the peace that would result from this kind of letting go? No matter what comes into our day, we relinquish our desire to strike back, to vindicate, to look good, to shame another, to let anger take hold, to have our own way. I get so bogged down in the frustrating specifics of life that I lose sight of the goal of life: *to become more like Christ.* As long as I see myself as a slave to the whims and moods of others, I will sink in the slough of despond. But when I let go and trust that God is totally in control, I can fly—even with broken wings.

This is a beautiful picture of childlike trust. I am not there yet, but I am beginning to get it. How happy it must make God when one of his children lives and loves with this level of understanding and grace.

David, thank you.

What a witness.

> Therefore, since we are surrounded by such a great cloud of witnesses, let us throw off everything that hinders and the sin that so easily entangles, and let us run with perseverance the race marked out for us. Let us fix our eyes on Jesus, the author and perfecter of our faith, who for the joy set before him endured the cross, scorning its shame, and sat down at the right hand of the throne of God.
>
> *Hebrews 12:1–2*

A CRY OF TRIUMPH

In the old classic *A Christian's Secret of a Happy Life,* Hannah Whitall Smith writes about "the lovely will of God."

She describes her love affair with God as if describing the best meal at an exquisite French restaurant. "The will of God is the most delicious and delightful thing in the universe," she says.

The fragrance of Christ in Hannah is a different perfume from any I have breathed in from anyone else. It's light and full of hallelujahs. She paints a canvas of the infinite unselfishness of God, which makes the will of God a pillow to rest on rather than a load to carry. It's clear that to Hannah there is no greater privilege on this earth than for a human heart to cry, "Thy will be done." It is a cry of triumph.

One theme keeps singing to me as I write: *We live to Christ; we live for one another.* I see it in my own home. William is about to turn eighty-two; he has recently lost his wife. And yet he describes his life at the moment as "the best days of my life." What is it that would evoke such a wonderful proclamation? It certainly isn't my cooking!

Part of it is obvious. He lives with his only son, whom he loves dearly, and his only grandson, whom he indulges copiously! He and I are good friends too. I love him very much. But there is more at work here. We are learning together how to live in community as those who treasure the hearts and spirits of one another. We get it wrong a lot, but we always say "sorry," sooner or later, and repair our bridges. We are learning that the corporate good is bigger than what each individual wants.

Now, before you suspect me of a refined kind of communism, let me expand a little. If we accept as basic premises that God is in control and that God is good, then it is not the responsibility of others to make us happy. Life is so much bigger than that. In our home we all make room for the things that bring us joy. We are not a house of martyrs, but we are learning to relinquish our so-called rights in order to love each other well. The amazing thing is that when we all fly in

A FEARLESS PRAYER

O that with yonder sacred throng
We at his feet may fall!
We'll join the everlasting song,
And crown him Lord of all;
We'll join the everlasting song,
And crown him Lord of all.
*   Amen.*

*   John Rippon*

9

HE IS FAITHFUL

Day by day, dear God, of you three things we pray:
to see you more clearly,
love you more dearly,
follow you more nearly,
day by day.

Richard of Chichester

From the fullness of his grace we have all received one blessing after
another. For the law was given through Moses; grace and truth
came through Jesus Christ.

John 1:16–17

And in his will is our peace.

Dante Alighieri

O come, let us adore him!

Knowing I'm about to go out of town again for a few days, I decide to use my last day in the office to the fullest and keep my nose to the grindstone. Barry says he'll take Christian to the mall to ride the carousel. I put on a fresh pot of coffee and settle into the rhythm of joyful work.

The phone rings. I consider letting the answering machine pick up, but I hate that. It feels like one more layer of protection to put between myself and real life. I pick up the phone.

It's one of my best friends. "You leave tomorrow?" she asks.

"Yes."

"Early?"

"About 8:00 A.M."

"Oh. Okay."

I hear her voice—and something more. "Do you want to get together for coffee now?" I ask.

"That would be great. Thanks."

The moment I see her, I recognize that look in her eyes. I've seen it so many times before in her—and in myself. The look of one dragging the burden of the shame of life through the town square while people stare. We discuss some minor incident in which those closest to her judged that her behavior didn't measure up and delivered the much-passed-around fruitcake of shame to her door. You know the one. We've all had it. No one knows what to do with it. It's so very heavy, and so we just keep passing it on to someone else.

As I look at her, I can see she's tired and sick of life, sick of her husband, sick of herself. I want to take her out to a field where the flowers are new and the spring rain falls gently and gently pluck this "stuff" off her. She is a beautiful person. She has a heart large enough to accommodate the woes and weariness of several countries. But the overcoat of shame is so familiar to her that whenever it's handed to her, she puts it on without question.

I listen as she pours out her cup of sadness. We talk. We laugh. We hug each other, and we remember. We remember that this "stuff" is temporary and that God is good.

How we all need the grace of God, I think. *How we need the faithful grace of God.*

At Women of Faith conferences the worship team typically sings a chorus called "But for Your Grace." They usually sing it before the speakers come onto the stage, so I hear it from backstage. But a few weeks ago they sang their songs in a different order, and we were present for this song. As I listened from this vantage point, I realized I had been singing the wrong words for a year. The lyrics are:

> *But for your grace I would not be saved,*
> *But for your grace I would go my way.*

I couldn't believe it. I had been singing:

> *But for your grace I would not be saved,*
> *But for your grace I would go insane.*

I got some of the words wrong, but the version I sang is so true for me. Without the grace of God I couldn't survive in this world. It was the faithful grace of God that breathed life back into me when others would have left me for dead and I would have considered it a mercy to be gone from this world. It was the faithful grace of God that held my hand as I watched Christian lying in an incubator as a three-day-old baby with suspicious blood problems. It was the faithful grace of God that walked the floors of my home with me that night as I waited for the results of another test on my then-three-year-old son. It's the faithful grace of God that gives Brian and Debbie and Taylor a place to throw themselves and beat their hands on the chest of God and get up again and go for one more round of experimental medication. It's the grace of God. The faithful grace of God.

But for your grace I would go insane.

Barry and I sit in our counselor's office. We have booked a two-hour session, so the therapist knows we have "stuff" to deal with. We talk about the Ghana thing. We know it's more than the Ghana thing. Barry finally confesses that the bottom line is that he's afraid something will happen to me and I won't come home. Loving makes us so vulnerable.

Our counselor asks him if he is ashamed of this fear.

"Well, sure," he admits. "As a Christian man I'm not supposed to feel that. God has called Sheila, and I know I need to trust him to take care of all of us."

This is our human dilemma. We know what we are supposed to be—and we know we're not—so we pretend to be, and it nearly kills us. Grace welcomes us to sit alone with God and unwrap all that's true about us, confident that he will not say, "You did what! What is wrong with you!" Jesus has been there before us. He took the massive debt of our sin and settled the bill. Remember the two lost sons? Remember Flora Campbell and her father Lachlan? Even when we are faithless, he is faithful.

> I remember my affliction and my wandering,
> > the bitterness and the gall.
> I well remember them,
> > and my soul is downcast within me.
> Yet this I call to mind
> > and therefore I have hope:
> Because of the LORD's great love we are not consumed,
> > for his compassions never fail.
> They are new every morning;
> > great is your faithfulness.
>
> *Lamentations 3:19–23*

TOO GOOD TO BE TRUE?

George MacDonald was a great Scottish preacher and writer. I've read that when he was telling his son about the grace of God and the glories of our future life, the boy said that it was just too good to be true. George replied, "Nay, laddie. It's just so good it *must* be true!"

God's faithfulness and grace make the impossible possible. I see it in my friend Thelma Wells. When you listen to her story, you can't help but think she should be a bitter, angry, defeated woman. But she's not. She was born the illegitimate daughter of a young, crippled black girl. Thelma was not welcomed into the world. Her grandmother was ashamed of her and would leave her in a dark closet for hours at a time. As she grew up, she faced the worst kind of racial humiliation and bigotry. She was bodily thrown out of a secretarial college on the first day of registration because of the color of her skin.

But into that cruel world, God extended to Thelma a gift of grace. Her great-grandmother loved her fiercely. Granny was a conduit of the love and grace of God to this young, unwelcomed child. God's faithfulness through Granny made the impossible possible. Instead of becoming a bitter, hard woman, Thelma is a magnificent lover of people. At every conference she has a long line of women who want to be hugged by her. As she wraps her arms around other people, it is a sacrament of grace in action. Only *God* could do that.

Grace gives us the opportunity to live now as we will live forever. When this life we cling to is over, we will only be beginning to live. Grace is getting what we do not deserve from the faithful hand of God. Just when we expect a slap, we receive a kiss. It's like Eliza Doolittle, only so much better.

Do you remember the story? It was popularized in the award-winning musical called *My Fair Lady*. The original play, written by George Bernard Shaw, is called *Pygmalion*. It's the story of two men who make a bet on which of them could take a common London street girl and transform her into a proper lady. Professor Higgins is sure he will be able to mold Eliza and pass her off to high society as a great lady. He works on her speech, trying to rid her of her Cockney accent. He works on her posture, her manners, her clothing. Then the great test: He takes Eliza to a ball. She looks like a princess and is greeted as such. He wins the bet.

Then he is done with her. She is devastated. She has nowhere to go. She doesn't belong in his world, but she can't go back to hers.

What Jesus Christ has done for us is something the best writers, producers, and directors could never come up with. He left all he had in order to come and embrace us in our filthy rags. He cleans us up—but doesn't leave us there. He takes us home to live with him forever. It's like the story of the Prodigal Son in reverse. Christ, the Son who had it all, came to us in a far country and gave up his inheritance for us. Now he stands at his Father's right hand as the elder brother, but as the one who *welcomes* us home—even though we were the ones who frittered away his inheritance. And with his Father he watches for us, and when he sees us on the horizon, he runs to welcome us home. Referring to Christ's return to heaven, Frere Pierre Marie says, from the perspective of the Father, "My Prodigal Son is home, and he has brought them all back with him!"

> After this I looked and there before me was a great multitude that no one could count, from every nation, tribe, people and language, standing before the throne and in front of the Lamb. They were wearing white robes and were holding palm branches in their hands. And they cried out in a loud voice:
>
> > "Salvation belongs to our God,
> > who sits on the throne,
> > and to the Lamb."
>
> All the angels were standing around the throne and around the elders and the four living creatures. They fell down on their faces before the throne and worshiped God, saying:
>
> > "Amen!
> > Praise and glory

and wisdom and thanks and honor
and power and strength
be to our God for ever and ever.
Amen!"

Revelation 7:9–12

COME! LET US ADORE HIM!

Worship. I have known the word since I was a child. Worship began at 11:00 every Sunday morning. But what does it really mean?

In *Mere Christianity* C. S. Lewis says that the test of true worship is that:

(a) you forget about yourself completely, or
(b) you see yourself as a small, filthy object

Lewis suggests that the first option is the one to choose: Forget about yourself.

But isn't worship all about *relationship*? If there is no real, honest relationship, it's impossible to worship in spirit and truth, as Jesus commanded us to (see John 4:24). So often the person we are least honest with is God, but he knows all about our "stuff"—and he loves us! Authentic worship flows out of telling the truth, out of facing our greatest fears, out of finding his peace in unexpected places.

Authentic worship flows out of telling the truth, out of facing our greatest fears, out of finding his peace in unexpected places.

Women of Faith had a conference in Denver, Colorado, in the fall of 1999, and it had been arranged for the six speakers to have lunch with some of the moms who had lost a child in the school shootings in Littleton. Quite honestly, I was nervous about this particular lunch. Being a mom has made me so much more tuned in to mothers whose children have died. What could I possibly say? I couldn't even begin to imagine such a horror.

I remember watching that harrowing event live on television, along with the rest of a stunned country, wondering what was happening to our world. I thought back to my high school days in Scotland, where the greatest tragedy was a fourteen-year-old girl getting pregnant. Now we were seeing children running out of classrooms, screaming for their lives, knowing that some of their best friends were lying behind them in pools of blood.

The networks kept showing one particular video clip—that of an injured boy covered with blood, climbing out of an upper window. I'm sure if you were watching television at any point during that week, you saw this clip. I remember praying for him, asking God to protect him so he would make it out safely. I wondered if his family was watching it too. I had no idea then that, a short while later, his mother would be one of the women to join us for lunch in Denver.

It was a little awkward at first. We introduced ourselves and sat around one long table. There were about fourteen women in all. Barbara Johnson was wonderful. Having buried two sons, she is able, in a way I never could, to touch parents who have lost children. I watched her relate in a loving, tender manner to each mom. She had brought gifts of her books for them, and she gave all of us a book on what it's like to face the first Christmas after the death of your child.

It was a lunch I will never forget. There were many tears shed, and, amazingly, there was much laughter too, as these women shared some of the funny and touching moments in the lives of their children. But it was the words of one of the mothers whose son was shot and killed in the school library that stayed with me—and always will.

She told us that she had waited outside the school for hours that day, hoping, praying. She knew her son was inside, but no one would confirm if he was among the dead. At eleven o'clock that night she was sent home, still not knowing, still not having seen her son.

"I was in shock when I got back to the house," she told us. "Numb. Cold. The house was full of people. I needed to be alone, so I got into the shower and turned the water on. It was the only place where I could go inside and lock the door. I prayed this prayer: 'Lord Jesus, if I'm going to get through this, I don't need to be one-quarter full of your Spirit, or even half full of your Spirit. I need to be filled to overflowing with your Spirit—one hundred percent. Protect my sanity. Protect my marriage.'"

I was stunned by the simple, profound wisdom of this terrified woman's whispered prayer. Instead of praying for God to change the circumstances, she prayed for God to change *her*. That's radical to me. At the point of the greatest horror a mother could experience, her prayer was that God would change her. First, she acknowledged God, even as her heart was full of dread. How else could she ever find peace? Then she confessed her inability to make it through without Christ. At this juncture in her life, from which point onward nothing would ever be the same, she was given a precious insight into her own soul.

Tragedy has a way of doing that. It holds up a mirror before us—and all masks fall away, revealing our true self. Joy can do that too. Unexpected good fortune. So can illness or depression. *Every* act upon the human stage will reveal to us what is in us *if* we are willing to take an honest look.

Personally, I fear that so much of our worship has become nothing more than spiritual-sounding *ya da ya da ya da*. We all live in a land of broken dreams and broken relationships, where we have forgotten how to tell the truth. We've forgotten how to say, with feeling:

God, I'm lost.
God, I don't know if you love me.
God, I'm afraid.
Lord Jesus Christ, Son of God, have mercy on me, a sinner.
God, I love you.
O come, let us adore him!

God doesn't ask us to worship him in spirit and in truth because he has forgotten who he is. No, God does not have Alzheimer's. He wants us to worship authentically because it changes *us*—*he* changes us. And he loves it when his children love him.

I was getting ready one evening to go out for dinner with Barry and our friends Steve and Marilyn. Christian came into the bedroom and said, "Mommy! You're beautiful!" What a gift! It's a picture of what worship really is. It's moving honestly through the pain and fear of life. It's washing off all the smudges we have put on the face of God and replacing them with a kiss. He has given all, and he is crazy about us. He is faithful, even when we are not. *God, you are beautiful!*

Annie Dillard writes that if you want to see the stars, you have to go outside. They don't *demand* your presence. They will shine anyway. But, if you want to see them, *you* have to move. It is the same with God's presence. He shines anyway, but we are changed by being in his presence.

We will never have all the answers down here. There are too many broken pieces. But we just keep walking, together, singing of his "Amazing Grace"! And in this grace, in the circle of this utter faithfulness that sustains us through both the wonderful and the horrible, we will find peace.

THIS TENDER BED OF SNOW

I am a winter person,
I have a winter soul.
Cold shades of silver gray and blue
Have stories to be told.
The riches from their bleakness,
Stripped down to barest bone,
Yet so alive
Though deep inside
This tender bed of snow.

Sheila Walsh

A Fearless Prayer

Lord!
How we love you.
This is no longer my book, my prayers.
There are too many of us for that.
We sing one song.
We love you.
And we say Yes!

Your Broken-Winged Flyers

10

ALL THAT MATTERS

To live with fear and not be afraid is the final test of maturity.
Edward Weeks

Praise the LORD, O my soul
and forget not all his benefits—
who forgives all your sins
and heals all your diseases,
who redeems your life from the pit
and crowns you with love and compassion,
who satisfies your desires with good things
so that your youth is renewed like the eagle's.
Psalm 103:2–5

Trust in him at all times, O people;
pour out your hearts to him,
for God is our refuge.

Psalm 62:8

Jesus loves me, this I know!

I was almost finished writing. I was ready to put the "Amen" to it and sleep for a week. But God was not quite finished with his spectacular array of shining stars. He had one more for me to meet.

I am the national spokesperson for House of Hope, a program for runaway and "throwaway" kids, based in Orlando, Florida. The ministry is headed up by one of the most amazing women I have ever met, Sara Trollinger. She never says, "Here, let me *tell* you how God loves you." Instead, with her whole life, she says, "Come, let me *show* you how God loves you."

God was not quite finished with his spectacular array of shining stars.

House of Hope began with two hundred dollars and a pure ambition, the purest I have ever seen. Now they have one of the most beautiful campuses for hurting kids. The teenagers who enter the program have been sexually abused, addicted to drugs and/or alcohol, or raped. Many have lived rough lives on the streets. Their stories are heartbreaking. Sara and her staff love them back to life—with Jesus' love. They love them with such a passion that, after just a few weeks, most of the kids want to know this radical Jesus, who is unlike anyone they have ever experienced before. Every time Barry and I visit we want to take half of these kids home with us.

We were in Florida in February of 2000 for their annual Humanitarian of the Year banquet. We came a couple of days early so we could take Christian to Walt Disney World and to Seuss Landing at Universal Studios Escape Islands of Adventure. I decided it would be good if Christian took a little nap before we set off for "round one" of the theme-park tour. Well, he slept for three hours! But when he finally woke up around 6:00 P.M., the hotel concierge informed us that the Magic Kingdom was open until ten that evening.

Christian went ballistic during the fifteen-minute cab ride over.

"Can I see Mickey first?"

"Yes."

"Will he remember me from last year?"

"I don't know, darling."

"I bet he will. I had on a cool hat. Will he kiss me and hug me and pat me?"

"I'm sure he will. How could he help himself? Look at you!"

We got there at twenty minutes to seven to discover that the concierge had it all wrong. The park was closing at seven. I couldn't believe it. Barry and I were almost in tears. We turned into manic parents.

"Can we pay the $200 just to say hello to Mickey?" The girl at the ticket counter told us that by the time we got on the tram and over to the park it would be closed.

"Is he here, Mom? Is he here?" Christian inquired frantically.

I told Barry I would take Christian to the gift shop by the ticket window till he came up with something. I was so upset for Christian that I temporarily lost my mind. I would have bought him whatever he wanted in the store. Mickey cigarettes, "Mickey Sings Heavy Metal," Mickey grenades. (Note to myself: *I must read a good Christian parenting book*.) Fortunately, all my boy wanted was a ball.

Barry and William came in with long faces. "There's nothing we can do, Babe," Barry said. Barry bought Christian a stuffed Mickey, and William bought him a watch.

Just then the girl at the ticket window came running in. "I have a great idea!" she said. "Take him over to Downtown Disney. They have a place where he can have his photo taken with Mickey!"

We kissed her. We hugged her. She is named in our wills. We got in another cab and set off.

It was so perfect! There were no other children there when we arrived, so Christian had Mickey all to himself. The big mouse hugged him and kissed him, high-fived him, and danced with him. Then he autographed a photo for him. It was so much better than what we had planned. I knew there was a life lesson there, but I was too tired to think it through just then.

The next day Christian posed with The Cat in the Hat and The Grinch. We did it all—and more—and fell into our beds late on Friday night. I knew I had a brunch to attend the next morning. *I wonder if I need to go?* I thought. *I could tell them I have theme-park disease.*

The event started at eleven. Sara seated me at a table with seven others. The woman beside me introduced herself as Debbie Arden. She jumped right in.

"You will never know how God has used you to help me, Sheila. I came to your conference last summer in Orlando. The only thing I bought was your *Hope* CD."

"Thanks! I loved making that one. Celtic music is my heritage."

"I know. I've been in your hometown."

I wondered if she meant Nashville, so I asked her.

"No! I mean Ayr, Scotland."

"You've been to Ayr? No one has been to Ayr!"

"Well, I have, and I loved it. My husband was Payne Stewart's golf agent. Payne was playing the course at Troon, and on my one day off I went to Ayr."

My mind began to spin. I am not a golfer, but I knew that Payne Stewart had been killed recently in a plane crash. Debbie must have seen the question in my eyes.

"Yes, my husband, Van, was on the plane too."

I didn't know what to say. She saw the sadness in my eyes.

"Sheila, you can never know the goodness of God to me in all of this. I was not in a great place with God before Van's death. I was overworked, stressed, anxious, finding it hard to pray. God took the death of my husband and, as Oswald Chambers said, used it as a pinhole to let me behold the face of God.

"I bought your music in June. Van was killed in October. I had no idea how much I would need it. I listened to it a couple of times right after I bought it, but since I don't have a CD player in my car, that was it. But I came home from Van's memorial service and played it constantly for two weeks. I played it from morning until morning. You walked with me through the worst days of my life. God filled all my dark places with his love and hope—so much so that I never said 'Why?' I only said 'What?' 'What do you want to say to me, Lord? I'm listening.'"

One more time I wanted to get up on the highest mountain and kiss God's beautiful face. Can you imagine such a thing? Can you take in this scene—that at the most heartbreaking moment of a woman's life, God would fill the cracks with himself?

I asked Debbie if she was surprised by how she'd responded.

"If you had told me that my husband was about to go down in a terrifying air crash, I would have told you that I would disappear under the covers and never come out. I would have known that I would sink into a deep, dark hole and never come out again. *I* would have known that. But God ... But God ... How can I put it into words?"

There was no need. It was written in bold print all over her.

Even as I sat with this new friend, I felt my own fear dissipate. I felt my own terror about the "what ifs?" take a seat further back in the arena of my heart. It didn't leave the building. I'm not sure it ever will. But it's no longer in a front-row seat. It does not have a guest pass.

This is one of my greatest challenges as a woman, as a mother. I acknowledge that for me, fear will always be part of life. I cannot imagine reaching a place where I am not afraid of anything anymore as long as I am on this earth, the broken side of eternity. But it does not have to overwhelm the whole melody of life. It will be there like an instrument in the orchestra, like the soulful deep cry of the cello that rests in the basement of the music. Its presence seems to make the other strings, the woodwind, the piano even more beautiful. To live with fear and faith, to hear faith say Yes! more often than fear, is one of the great joys and marks of our calling.

To live with fear and faith, to hear faith say Yes! more often than fear, is one of the great joys and marks of our calling.

You must know this: I don't write about things I understand. I write about things I *want* to understand. When I began the process of writing this book, I was in a different place than I am now. I have been welcomed into the private rooms of so many who have lived out my fears in front of me and who are still here, still loving and serving God. I believe they love him even more than when they were "intact." Do I welcome this pain into *my* life, or do I wish it on *them*? Absolutely not! But what I carry with me now is threefold:

> It is the assurance that God will do what we cannot do;
> that he will be there to speak into unspeakable situations;
> that we need one another to live.

It's not that we have all the right words or enough wisdom to heal deep wounds; it's just that we are there.

I saw this again this morning. Brian Schrauger had e-mailed me in Florida. The news on Taylor was bad. He was in so much pain. I returned Brian's e-mail:

> I can't imagine.
> It makes me sick to even try to.
> I can think of nothing good to say.

> Your sister,
> Sheila

Brian's reply was beautiful:

> Actually, Sheila, in my grade book your encouraging, empathetic words deserve an A+.
>
> > Thank you.

I cringe to think what I would have written a few years ago. I would have wanted to do the right thing and say the right thing. But when someone's child is in agony, fighting for his life, there is *no* right thing. Part of the fear of facing suffering head-on is that we won't know what to do or say. I say *just show up*. Most of the time, show up and shut up. Weep. Hug. Love. Pray. Weep some more. Help to carry the broken glass of humanity without looking for gloves to protect yourself.

In the Presence of the Lord

I got back to the hotel after the House of Hope brunch and opened a gift that Debbie Arden had given me. She is an artist, and she had painted in watercolors the words and the scene of Psalm 103:5: "who satisfies your desires with good things so that your youth is renewed like the eagle's."

I read her note:

> I have always loved Celtic music. It is to me a picture of how God can take even the sorrowful, melancholy beats of my heart and bring them into cadence with his, resulting in—somehow—praise and joy. Even when the burdens are heavy, his burden is light, and I gladly choose it.
>
> > You are precious to me,
> > Debbie

Debbie, you are precious to me. You are precious to us. You are precious to God.

She included the verse from the devotional she found on Van's desk the day his ashes came home. "So with you: Now is your time of grief, but I will see you again and you will rejoice, and no one will take away your joy" (John 16:22).

Jesus loves me! this I know,
For the Bible tells me so;
Little ones to him belong,
They are weak but he is strong.
Yes, Jesus loves me!
Yes, Jesus loves me!
Yes, Jesus loves me!
The Bible tells me so.

So here we are—here in this parade of witnesses. And here is the truth as I see it now about this life we are called to live: It is painful. At times it is lonely. It's scary. It's unknown. But ... But ... Here in all his wonderful grace and glory stands God. He stands up in broken places. He stands up in broken people. He stands firm on bloodied feet. He stands among us.

Until then, how shall we live?

As I have watched those who have lost and yet who love, I am reminded that we are those who see through a glass darkly, who see but a poor reflection. When we finally see face-to-face, we, with the prophet Isaiah, will fall on our faces, bowled over by the sight. Until then, how shall we live?

I love the words of Mother Teresa:

People are often unreasonable, illogical, and self-centered;
Forgive them anyway.

If you are kind, people may accuse you of selfish, ulterior motives;
Be kind anyway.

If you are successful, you will win some false friends and some true enemies;
Succeed anyway.

If you are honest and frank, people may cheat you;
Be honest and frank anyway.

What you spend years building, someone could destroy overnight;
Build anyway.

If you find serenity and happiness, they may be jealous;
Be happy anyway.

The good you do today, people will often forget tomorrow;
Do good anyway.

Give the world the best you have, and it may never be enough;
Give the world the best you've got anyway.

You see, in the final analysis, it is between you and God;
It was never between you and them anyway.

Between you and God—with the Jesus who loves you in the middle. One day this is all that will matter. Really, it's all that matters now. When we truly understand it's all that matters, everything changes. Everything that matters to us matters to God; everything that matters to him matters to us.

We live in a world raw with fear, even consumed by fear. As believers we have so much to offer in our bruised, redeemed flesh to those who wail outside the city gates, alone. I love Paul's prayer: "Pray also for me, that whenever I open my mouth, words may be given me so that I will fearlessly make known the mystery of the gospel" (Ephesians 6:19). I make this prayer my very own.

As you read these final words, you may be in the midst of the darkest storm of your life. Come back with me to my favorite psalm, which I meditate on regularly:

The LORD is my light and my salvation—
  whom shall I fear?
The LORD is the stronghold of my life—
  of whom shall I be afraid?

Psalm 27:1

Until we stand before the throne of God, fear will always be present in this world. We welcome that day to come, echoing the final words of Scripture: "Amen. Come, Lord Jesus." Until then I will stand with you—fearlessly!

Will you stand with me?

EPILOGUE

Love always asks in the end that you be willing to let it turn to sorrow, and that you let that sorrow bear you all the way down to the very bottom of its poverty.

Jerome A. Miller

I woke up early on May 31, 2000, and went out onto the deck with that first wonderful cup of coffee. Our home looks out on the sixteenth hole of a golf course. It was quiet at the moment, but it would soon be a patchwork quilt of activity.

I love to sit and watch the golfers as they play. There are those keen players who concentrate as if they were performing brain surgery. Christian usually picks those moments to shout out, "Hey, golfers! Hello there, golfers!" They don't appreciate this at all. Some talk and laugh as they play ... and then there is that one woman. She usually comes by just before sunset. I try not to miss her. She is the worst golfer I've ever seen. She never gets any better, but she never gives up. On a good day she'll hit the ball about ten yards. Her balls end up in our yard, in the neighbor's flowers, in the pond. I am fascinated by this woman. I am tempted at times to have tea and sandwiches ready for her. *Would refreshments help?* I wonder.

I went inside and poured myself another cup of coffee. I heard the phone ring and wondered who would be calling this early. It was my friend Steve Lorenz. He told me Taylor had died at 5:20 A.M. I thanked him for letting me know and went back onto the deck and wept. I sobbed and sobbed. Not for Taylor now—he was home free. His battle was fierce beyond belief, but he was Home. My thoughts were with his parents, Brian and Debbie, with his brothers, Christopher and Jonathan.

I drove to their house. The boys were with friends. Brian had gone out to make some arrangements, but Debbie was home. She looked exhausted. Her face was white and drawn. She was so thin and fragile I felt I would break her if I hugged her too tightly.

Taylor's last hours were not what his family had prayed for. When it became clear that God was not going to physically heal him, they prayed for a smooth passing, a gentle crossing of the river. It wasn't like that. Taylor was afraid. As Brian held him in those last hours, he cried out:

Where am I?
Am I dying?
I feel like I'm falling.
What am I supposed to do?
Help me right now! Where are you?

Then a still moment—when he quietly said, "Taylor." It was as though someone had been asking him his name. A few moments later his battle was over. He was Home ... with two good legs. He celebrated his twelfth birthday with Christ.

Like my golfing friend, Taylor never quit. No matter how hard the path or how apparently fruitless the effort, he never gave up on life.

Brian wrote a letter to Taylor, reflecting on the last hours of his warrior son's life:

Taylor, sweetheart, you are perfectly safe. Dad is right here. So are Mom and Christopher. And best of all, Jesus is too. We're not going anywhere. And because we're all here, nothing bad can happen to you. We simply won't let it.

You are not going to die. Jesus already did that for you. And because he did, all that lies ahead of you is *life*. Life and life alone.

And so, buddy, there are only two things you need to do: Remember you are loved. And just go to sleep. After all, you can't wake up until you go to sleep!

During the battle I whispered in your ear, "I love you. Mom loves you. Christopher and Jonathan love you. You know that, right?" In a small voice you replied, "Yes."

"And Jesus loves you. You know that too, don't you?" In a somewhat exasperated tone you whispered, "Well, yeah!" Like, "Come on, Dad. Duh! Of course I know that!"

"Well, then," I answered with a grin, "when you remember that you're loved, it's impossible to stay scared."

It took awhile, but eventually fear did lose.

And when, at last, your beautiful old bod breathed its last, you left it with a smile. You actually left it with your beautiful, famous "Mona Lisa" smile. At the end, you knew that, really, your life had only just begun. Everything I said, everything God promised, was true.

Taylor's last cries were, as Brian wrote in an e-mail message two days after his son's death, "familiar cries of my own troubled soul."

Where am I?
Am I dying?
I feel like I'm falling.
What am I supposed to do?
Help me right now! Where are you, God?

The answer comes back, sometimes with a whisper, sometimes with a shout, "I am here. I am right here. I am here."

The LORD is my light and my salvation—
    whom shall I fear?
The LORD is the stronghold of my life—
    of whom shall I be afraid?

Psalm 27:1

Taylor Belon Schrauger

June 4, 1988 – May 31, 2000

HONESTLY
Sheila Walsh

Talented and beautiful, Sheila Walsh seemed to be on top of her world. But behind her public success as a performing artist and talk show host, a private story was unfolding.

Honestly takes you on a journey past the walls that most of us put up and into the recesses of one woman's heart. With rare grace, Sheila shares the story of her pilgrimage—the journey of a soul as it moved from hopelessness to honesty, to freedom, and, ultimately, to a deepened faith and joy. With refreshing candor, Sheila probes beyond the surface of her troubles to find a truth strong and real enough to set her free.

Honestly shows how facing the things about ourselves that we try hardest to hide—fearful specters of loss, shame, and doubt—puts us on the high road to God's liberating love and grace.

Hardcover 0-310-20325-2   Softcover 0-310-21916-7   Audio Pages 0-310-20486-0

Also available from Sheila Walsh

BRING BACK THE JOY
Rekindling the Joy in Your Relationship with God
Hardcover 0-310-22023-8   Softcover 0-310-22915-4

GIFTS FOR YOUR SOUL
A Book of Daily Devotions
Hardcover 0-310-20975-7

LOVE FALLS DOWN
Sheila Walsh
Integrity Music

Available February 2001

Celtic melodies with a mixture of contemporary and pop styling make *Love Falls Down* an album that will delight and intrigue you. With songs like "Where Truth and Mercy Meet" and "Your Love Falls Down," Sheila Walsh reminds us that God's eternal love can make a lasting difference in our lives.

ISBN: 0076-818822